C000246738

2019 SQA Specimen and Past Papers with Answers

National 5

MODERN STUDIES

2018 & 2019 Exams
and 2017 Specimen Question Paper

Hodder Gibson Study Skills Advice – National 5 Modern Studies	– page 3
Hodder Gibson Study Skills Advice – General	– page 5
2017 SPECIMEN QUESTION PAPER	– page 7
2018 EXAM	– page 25
2019 EXAM	– page 43
ANSWERS	– page 63

HODDER
GIBSON
AN HACHETTE UK COMPANY

12. Be an expert.

Be sure to have a few areas in which you feel you are an expert. This often works because at least some of them will come up, which can boost confidence.

13. Try some visual methods.

Use symbols, diagrams, charts, flashcards, post-it notes etc. Don't forget – the brain takes in chunked images more easily than loads of text.

14. Remember – practice makes perfect.

Work on difficult areas again and again. Look and read – then test yourself. You cannot do this too much.

15. Try past papers against the clock.

Practise writing answers in a set time. This is a good habit from the start but is especially important when you get closer to exam time.

16. Collaborate with friends.

Test each other and talk about the material – this can really help. Two brains are better than one! It is amazing how talking about a problem can help you solve it.

17. Know your weaknesses.

Ask your teacher for help to identify what you don't know. Try to do this as early as possible. If you are having trouble, it is probably with a difficult topic, so your teacher will already be aware of this – most students will find it tough.

18. Have your materials organised and ready.

Know what is needed for each exam:

- Do you need a calculator or a ruler?
- Should you have pencils as well as pens?
- Will you need water or paper tissues?

19. Make full use of school resources.

Find out what support is on offer:

- Are there study classes available?
- When is the library open?
- When is the best time to ask for extra help?
- Can you borrow textbooks, study guides, past papers, etc.?
- Is school open for Easter revision?

20. Keep fit and healthy!

Try to stick to a routine as much as possible, including with sleep. If you are tired, sluggish or dehydrated, it is difficult to see how concentration is even possible. Combine study with relaxation, drink plenty of water, eat sensibly, and get fresh air and exercise – all these things will help more than you could imagine. Good luck!

NATIONAL 5

2017 Specimen
Question Paper

National Qualifications 2017

S849/75/11

Modern Studies

Date — Not applicable

Duration — 2 hours 20 minutes

Total marks — 80

SECTION 1 — DEMOCRACY IN SCOTLAND AND THE UNITED KINGDOM — 28 marks

Attempt **EITHER** Part A **AND** Question 7 **OR** Part B **AND** Question 7

Part A   Democracy in Scotland   Pages 2—3

Part B   Democracy in the United Kingdom   Pages 4—5

Question 7   Pages 6—7

SECTION 2 — SOCIAL ISSUES IN THE UNITED KINGDOM — 26 marks

Attempt **EITHER** Part C **AND** Question 14 **OR** Part D **AND** Question 14

Part C   Social Inequality   Page 8

Part D   Crime and the Law   Page 9

Question 14   Pages 10—11

SECTION 3 — INTERNATIONAL ISSUES — 26 marks

Attempt **EITHER** Part E **AND** Question 21 **OR** Part F **AND** Question 21

Part E   World Powers   Page 12

Part F   World Issues   Page 13

Question 21   Pages 14—15

Write your answers clearly in the answer booklet provided. In the answer booklet you must clearly identify the question number you are attempting.

Use **blue** or **black** ink.

Before leaving the examination room you must give your answer booklet to the Invigilator; if you do not, you may lose all the marks for this paper.

MARKS

SECTION 1 — DEMOCRACY IN SCOTLAND AND THE UNITED KINGDOM — 28 marks

Attempt **EITHER** Part A **AND** Question 7 **OR** Part B **AND** Question 7

Part A   Democracy in Scotland   Pages 2—3

Part B   Democracy in the United Kingdom   Pages 4—5

Question 7   Pages 6—7

PART A — DEMOCRACY IN SCOTLAND

In your answers to Questions 1, 2 and 3 you should give recent examples from Scotland.

Question 1

In Scottish Parliament elections, political parties campaign in many ways.

Describe, **in detail**, **two** ways that political parties campaign in Scottish Parliament elections.

4

Question 2

The Scottish Parliament has responsibility for devolved matters.

Describe, **in detail**, **two** devolved matters for which the Scottish Parliament has responsibility.

6

Attempt **EITHER** Question 3(a) **OR** 3(b) on *Page three*

MARKS

Attempt **EITHER** Question 3(a) **OR** 3(b)

Question 3

(a)

The Additional Member System (AMS) has several advantages.

Explain, **in detail**, the advantages of the Additional Member System (AMS).

You should give a **maximum** of **three** advantages in your answer.   **8**

OR

(b)

People in Scotland can participate in society in many ways.

Explain, **in detail**, why some people in Scotland participate in one of the following:

- Pressure Groups
- Trade Unions.

You should give a **maximum** of **three** reasons in your answer.   **8**

[Now go to Question 7 starting on *Page six*]

PART B — DEMOCRACY IN THE UNITED KINGDOM

In your answers to Questions 4, 5 and 6 you should give recent examples from the United Kingdom.

Question 4

In General Elections, political parties campaign in many ways.

Describe, **in detail, two** ways political parties campaign during General Elections.

4

Question 5

The UK Parliament has responsibility for reserved matters in Scotland.

Describe, **in detail**, **two** reserved matters for which the UK Parliament has responsibility.

6

Attempt **EITHER** Question 6(a) **OR** 6(b) on *Page five*

MARKS

Attempt **EITHER** Question 6(a) **OR** 6(b)

Question 6

(a)

> First Past the Post has several disadvantages.

Explain, **in detail,** the disadvantages of First Past the Post.

You should give a **maximum** of **three** disadvantages in your answer.

8

OR

(b)

> People in the UK can participate in society in many ways.

Explain, **in detail**, why some people in the UK participate in one of the following:

- Pressure Groups
- Trade Unions.

You should give a **maximum** of **three** reasons in your answer.

8

[**Now go to Question 7 starting on** *Page six*]

Question 7

Study Sources 1, 2 and 3 and then answer the question which follows.

SOURCE 1

Composition of the House of Lords

The House of Commons and the House of Lords make up the two Chambers in the UK Parliament. In recent years, some changes have been made to the composition of the Lords. In 1995, over half of those who sat in the House of Lords were hereditary peers (this means they inherited their seat in the Lords from their father). The total number of Lords has changed and currently there are about 790 members, none of whom are directly elected by the public.

By 1997, about 36% of the House of Lords were appointed as a Lord for the length of their life (a life peer). Today, approximately 90% of Lords are life peers. Many Lords bring great experience and expertise to Parliament in the fields of medicine, law, business, science, sport and education, to name a few areas.

Although women have only been allowed to sit in the House of Lords since 1958, the Lord Speaker's role which was created in 2006 was initially held by two female peers, Baroness Hayman (2006-2011) and Baroness D'Souza (2011-2016). It is the Lord Speaker's job to oversee the business in the House of Lords. Lord Fowler, the current Lord Speaker, became the first man to occupy the position in 2016.

In the House of Lords, since 2000, 36% of newly appointed members have been women, 21% have been ethnic minorities and 10% have been disabled.

SOURCE 2

Comparison of selected factors in the House of Lords and the UK population

	House of Lords		UK population	
	1995	**2015**	**1995**	**2015**
Male	93%	75%	49%	49%
Female	7%	25%	51%	51%
Ethnic-minority background	Less than 1%	5%	6%	13%
% under 60 years of age	22%	16%	81%	77%
Average age	79	70	36	40
Privately educated	62%	50%	7%	7%
Graduated from Oxford or Cambridge University	35%	38%	Less than 1%	Less than 1%
Disabled	2%	11%	12%	17%

SOURCE 3

MARKS

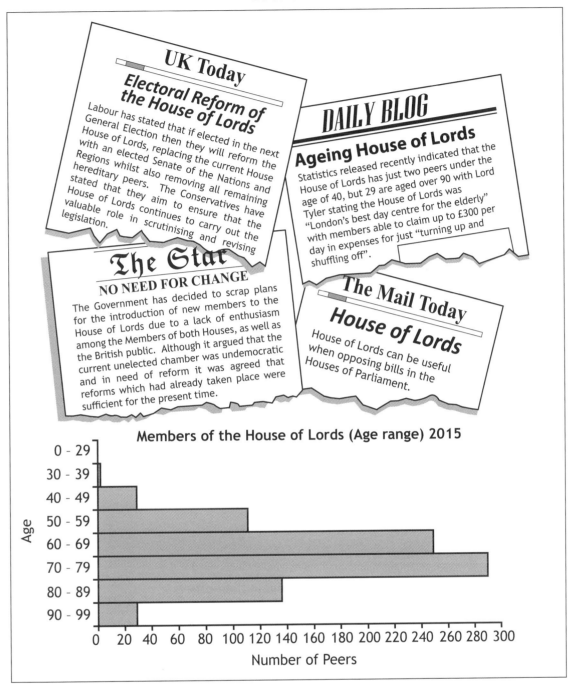

UK Today

Electoral Reform of the House of Lords

Labour has stated that if elected in the next General Election then they will reform the House of Lords, replacing the current House with an elected Senate of the Nations and Regions whilst also removing all remaining hereditary peers. The Conservatives have stated that they aim to ensure that the House of Lords continues to carry out the valuable role in scrutinising and revising legislation.

DAILY BLOG

Ageing House of Lords

Statistics released recently indicated that the House of Lords has just two peers under the age of 40, but 29 are aged over 90 with Lord Tyler stating the House of Lords was "London's best day centre for the elderly" with members able to claim up to £300 per day in expenses for just "turning up and shuffling off".

The Star

NO NEED FOR CHANGE

The Government has decided to scrap plans for the introduction of new members to the House of Lords due to a lack of enthusiasm among the Members of both Houses, as well as the British public. Although it argued that the current unelected chamber was undemocratic and in need of reform it was agreed that reforms which had already taken place were sufficient for the present time.

The Mail Today

House of Lords

House of Lords can be useful when opposing bills in the Houses of Parliament.

Members of the House of Lords (Age range) 2015

Age	Number of Peers
0 – 29	
30 – 39	~2
40 – 49	~35
50 – 59	~110
60 – 69	~245
70 – 79	~290
80 – 89	~135
90 – 99	~30

Using Sources 1, 2 and 3, give reasons to support and oppose the view of Morag Watt.

> The House of Lords is in need of further reform.
>
> **View of Morag Watt**

In your answer you **must**:

- give evidence from the sources that supports Morag Watt's view

and

- give evidence from the sources that opposes Morag Watt's view.

Your answer **must** be based on all **three** sources.

10

NOW GO TO SECTION 2 ON *Page eight*

SECTION 2 — SOCIAL ISSUES IN THE UNITED KINGDOM — 26 marks

MARKS

Attempt **EITHER** Part C **AND** Question 14 **OR** Part D **AND** Question 14

Part C   Social Inequality   Page 8

Part D   Crime and the Law   Page 9

Question 14   Pages 10–11

PART C — SOCIAL INEQUALITY

In your answers to Questions 8, 9 and 10 you should give recent examples from the United Kingdom.

Question 8

Groups that experience inequality in the UK		
Women	Ethnic Minorities	Elderly

Choose **one** of the groups above **or any other group** you have studied.

Describe, **in detail**, **two** ways the Government has tried to reduce the inequalities experienced by the group you have chosen.

4

Question 9

Some people in the UK have a better standard of living than others.

Explain, **in detail**, **two** reasons why some people in the UK have a better standard of living than others.

6

Question 10

There are many groups in the UK which experience social and economic inequality.

Explain, **in detail**, **two** reasons why one or more groups you have studied experience social and economic inequality in the UK.

6

[Now go to Question 14 starting on *Page ten*]

PART D — CRIME AND THE LAW

In your answers to Questions 11, 12 and 13 you should give recent examples from the United Kingdom.

Question 11

Groups that tackle crime in the UK		
Government	Police	Courts

Choose **one** of the groups above.

Describe, **in detail**, **two** ways in which the group you have chosen has tried to tackle crime in the UK.

4

Question 12

Some people are affected by crime more than others.

Explain, **in detail**, **two** reasons why some people are affected by crime more than others.

6

Question 13

There are many factors which cause crime in the UK.

Explain, **in detail**, **two** factors which cause crime in the UK.

6

[Now go to Question 14 starting on *Page ten*]

Question 14

Study Sources 1, 2 and 3 and then answer the question which follows.

You are a government adviser. You have been asked to recommend **whether** or **not** the United Kingdom Government should ban Legal Highs.

Option 1	Option 2
Ban Legal Highs	Do not ban Legal Highs

SOURCE 1

Legal Highs Factfile

The UK Government is currently examining legislation that will control the sale and use of "legal highs". A legal high contains one or more chemical substances which produce similar effects to illegal drugs, like cocaine, cannabis and ecstasy. These drugs are often included in everyday household products and are often labelled "not for human consumption". Legal highs are often seen as "designer drugs" and can be easily bought and sold online.

- Legal highs are currently not covered by the Misuse of Drugs Act, 1971.
- Some EU countries have already passed legislation controlling the sale and use of legal highs.
- There was a mass demonstration against the proposed legislation due to the inclusion of nitrous oxide, otherwise known as laughing gas, within the bill. Nitrous oxide is commonly used as an anaesthetic during dentistry, childbirth and as a mood enhancer.
- Legal highs have been linked to hospital admissions for things such as poisoning, mental health issues, and in extreme cases death.
- Despite the media attention, around half of young people have never experimented with legal highs.
- The government is looking at a bill that will make it illegal to sell any "psychoactive substances" other than alcohol, caffeine and nicotine.
- There has been little or no research into the long term or short term risks of taking legal highs.
- The UK has the most severe problem with legal highs in Western Europe, with significant numbers of young people regularly admitting to taking legal highs.
- Many health experts argue banning legal highs will not prevent people taking them; educating people on the danger of these substances would be more beneficial.
- Under the proposed legislation, possession will remain legal so long as there is no intent to supply. The bill could mean up to seven years in prison for people who provide drugs to others.

SOURCE 2

Survey of 16–25 year olds on legal highs

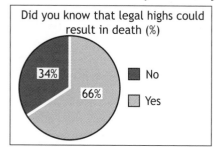

Did you know that legal highs could result in death (%)

34% No
66% Yes

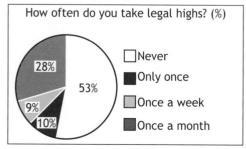

How often do you take legal highs? (%)

28%
53%
9%
10%

Never
Only once
Once a week
Once a month

MARKS

Question 14 (continued)

SOURCE 2 (continued)

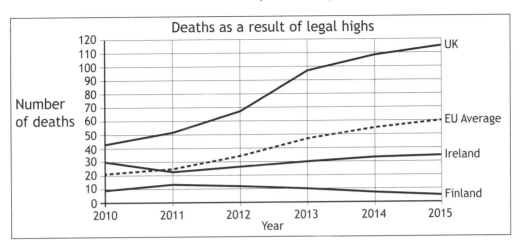

Deaths as a result of legal highs

SOURCE 3

Viewpoints

Control and monitoring of legal highs is very difficult. Current laws mean that decisions on whether a product is allowed to be sold are made on a case by case basis. Often new versions are created and sold just as fast as the government can ban them. This makes it difficult to monitor and police.

The government's plan for a blanket ban on legal highs is impractical and not supported by everyone. The Irish government banned legal highs after a number of deaths linked to their use; however this did not reduce deaths and was unsuccessful.

Anna Drummond, Youth Worker

More of my time as a paramedic is being taken up dealing with the consequences of legal highs. The misuse of these drugs diverts our attention from cases that are much more important.

Legal highs are becoming increasingly popular particularly among young people who assume "legal" means "safe". Young people have become much more aware of the health risks of illegal drugs and we see fewer young people addicted to drugs like heroin. However, lots of people are unaware of the dangers of legal highs.

Mandeep Khan, Paramedic

You must decide which option to recommend, **either** ban Legal Highs (**Option 1**) **or** do not ban Legal Highs (**Option 2**).

(i)   Using Sources 1, 2 and 3, **which option would you choose**?

(ii) Give reasons to **support** your choice.

(iii) **Explain** why you did not choose the other option.

Your answer must be based on all **three** sources.

10

NOW GO TO SECTION 3 ON *Page twelve*

SECTION 3 — INTERNATIONAL ISSUES — 26 marks

MARKS

Attempt **EITHER** Part E **AND** Question 21 **OR** Part F **AND** Question 21

Part E   World Powers   Page 12

Part F   World Issues   Page 13

Question 21   Pages 14–15

PART E — WORLD POWERS

In your answers to Questions 15, 16 and 17 you should give recent examples from a world power you have studied.

Question 15

> Governments have made many attempts to tackle social and economic inequality.

Describe, **in detail**, **two** ways in which the government has tried to tackle social and economic inequality.

In your answer you must state the world power you have studied.   4

Question 16

> The citizens of every world power have political rights.

Describe, **in detail**, **two** political rights that the citizens have in the world power you have studied.

In your answer you must state the world power you have studied.   6

Question 17

> World powers have the ability to influence other countries.

Explain, **in detail**, **two** reasons why the world power you have studied has the ability to influence other countries.

In your answer you must state the world power you have studied.   6

[Now go to Question 21 starting on *Page fourteen*]

MARKS

PART F — WORLD ISSUES

In your answers to Questions 18, 19 and 20 you should give recent examples from a world issue you have studied.

Question 18

International organisations which try to resolve international issues and problems		
United Nations Organisation	NATO	World Bank
European Union	African Union	Charities and other NGOs

Describe, **in detail**, **two** ways in which international organisations have tried to resolve an international issue or conflict you have studied.

In your answer you must state the world issue or conflict you have studied.   **4**

Question 19

People are affected by international conflicts and issues in many different ways.

Describe, **in detail**, **two** ways in which people have been affected by an international conflict or issue you have studied.

In your answer you must state the world issue or conflict you have studied.   **6**

Question 20

The attempts of international organisations to tackle conflicts and issues are sometimes unsuccessful.

Explain, **in detail**, **two** reasons why international organisations have **either** been successful **or** unsuccessful in tackling an international conflict or issue you have studied.

In your answer you must state the world issue or conflict you have studied.   **6**

[Now go to Question 21 starting on *Page fourteen*]

Question 21

Study Sources 1, 2 and 3 and then answer the question which follows.

SOURCE 1

Problems facing Japan in 2015

Many people think Japan is in crisis. Its problems include a weak economy and a rapidly changing population structure. All of these things are long term problems which are affecting Japanese standards of living.

Since the economic crisis that hit the world in 2008, low incomes have become a problem. It is estimated that 16% of all Japanese people are living below the poverty line. Average income went from 37,185 US dollars in 2008 to 34,822 US dollars in 2011.

One third of working age women now live in poverty. 12 million women in Japan work but over half are in part-time jobs, receiving small salaries. Part-time work helps those with families and school-age children but has a negative impact because it prevents many from having financial savings which is a major worry for Japanese women.

Increased poverty and a different population structure will make old age pensions and elderly care very expensive in the future. By the middle of this century over one third of the population will be collecting their old age pension.

Despite all the problems facing modern Japan, many people point to its strengths. It had 22 crimes per 1,000 people in 2014. It remains the third largest economy in the world where some people still enjoy an extremely high standard of living.

SOURCE 2

	People in poverty (%)	Crimes per 1000 people	Home ownership (%)	Internet access per 1000 people
Additional statistics – Selected Countries				
Germany	15	79	44	841
Argentina	30	36	67	599
South Korea	16·5	32	54	865
Italy	19·6	39	74	585
France	8	61	64	819
European Union	8	80	71	848

MARKS

SOURCE 2 (continued)

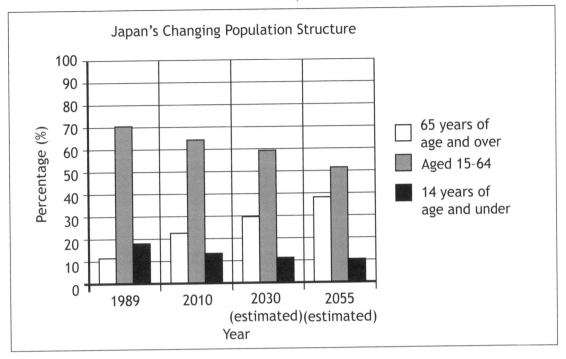

Japan's Changing Population Structure

Legend:
- 65 years of age and over
- Aged 15-64
- 14 years of age and under

X-axis: Year — 1989, 2010, 2030 (estimated), 2055 (estimated)
Y-axis: Percentage (%)

SOURCE 3

Better Life Index Study

According to the Better Life Index, citizens in Japan are not entirely happy.

Japanese women have an average happiness level of 4·67 (out of 10) whereas Japanese men have an average level of 6·21. However, happiness is not equal amongst all women. Working age women have a happiness level of 3·2 whilst 70-74 year olds have a level of 5·5.

Japan boasts one of the highest life expectancies in the world at 83 years. In future this may be difficult to maintain as the proportion of the population paying tax falls.

The country continues to be at the forefront of the electronics industry which employs many people. Of every 1000 Japanese people, 865 have access to the internet. Just over three quarters of Japanese people say they are satisfied with their home. 61% of Japanese people own their own homes but housing has become much more expensive for young people due to the growing numbers of older people.

Using Sources 1, 2 and 3, what **conclusions** can be drawn?

You should reach a conclusion about each of the following:

- The problem of crime in Japan compared to other countries.
- The effects of the changing population structure in Japan.
- The effect of poverty on working age women.
- The country most like Japan.

Your conclusions must be supported by evidence from the sources. You should link information within and between the sources in support of your conclusions.

Your answer **must** be based on all **three** sources.

10

[END OF SPECIMEN QUESTION PAPER]

[BLANK PAGE]

DO NOT WRITE ON THIS PAGE

NATIONAL 5

2018

National Qualifications 2018

X849/75/11

Modern Studies

WEDNESDAY, 9 MAY

1:00 PM — 3:20 PM

Total marks — 80

SECTION 1 — DEMOCRACY IN SCOTLAND AND THE UNITED KINGDOM — 28 marks

Attempt **EITHER** Part A **AND** question 7 **OR** Part B **AND** question 7

Part A   Democracy in Scotland   Pages 2—3

Part B   Democracy in the United Kingdom   Pages 4—5

Question 7   Pages 6—7

SECTION 2 — SOCIAL ISSUES IN THE UNITED KINGDOM — 26 marks

Attempt **EITHER** Part C **AND** question 14 **OR** Part D **AND** question 14

Part C   Social inequality   Page 8

Part D   Crime and the law   Page 9

Question 14   Pages 10—11

SECTION 3 — INTERNATIONAL ISSUES — 26 marks

Attempt **EITHER** Part E **AND** question 21 **OR** Part F **AND** question 21

Part E   World powers   Page 12

Part F   World issues   Page 13

Question 21   Pages 14—15

Write your answers clearly in the answer booklet provided. In the answer booklet you must clearly identify the question number you are attempting.

Use **blue** or **black** ink.

Before leaving the examination room you must give your answer booklet to the Invigilator; if you do not, you may lose all the marks for this paper.

MARKS

SECTION 1 — DEMOCRACY IN SCOTLAND AND THE UNITED KINGDOM — 28 marks

Attempt **EITHER** Part A **AND** question 7 **OR** Part B **AND** question 7

Part A   Democracy in Scotland   Pages 2—3

Part B   Democracy in the United Kingdom   Pages 4—5

Question 7   Pages 6—7

PART A — DEMOCRACY IN SCOTLAND

In your answers to questions 1, 2 and 3 you should give recent examples from Scotland.

Question 1

> MSPs can represent constituents in many different ways in the Scottish Parliament.

Describe, **in detail**, **two** ways in which MSPs can represent their constituents in the Scottish Parliament.

4

Question 2

> Groups use various methods to gain influence in a democracy.

Select one of the groups below:

- Pressure groups
- Trade unions.

Describe, **in detail, two** methods used by the group you have selected to gain influence in a democracy.

6

Attempt **EITHER** question 3(a) **OR** 3(b) on *Page three*

Attempt **EITHER** question 3(a) **OR** 3(b)

Question 3

(a)

> Many people in Scotland choose not to vote in elections.

Explain, **in detail**, why many people in Scotland choose not to vote in elections.

You should give a **maximum** of **three** reasons in your answer.   **8**

OR

(b)

> The First Minister is very powerful.

Explain, **in detail**, why the First Minister is very powerful.

You should give a **maximum** of **three** reasons in your answer.   **8**

[Now go to question 7 starting on *Page six*]

PART B — DEMOCRACY IN THE UNITED KINGDOM

In your answers to questions 4, 5 and 6 you should give recent examples from the United Kingdom.

Question 4

> MPs can represent constituents in many different ways in the UK Parliament.

Describe, **in detail**, **two** ways in which MPs can represent their constituents in the UK Parliament.

4

Question 5

> Groups use various methods to gain influence in a democracy.

Select one of the groups below:

- Pressure groups
- Trade unions.

Describe, **in detail**, **two** methods used by the group you have selected to gain influence in a democracy.

6

Attempt **EITHER** question 6(a) **OR** 6(b) on *Page five*

MARKS

Attempt EITHER question 6(a) OR 6(b)

Question 6

(a)

> Many people in the UK choose not to vote in elections.

Explain, **in detail**, why many people in the UK choose not to vote in elections.
You should give a **maximum** of **three** reasons in your answer.

8

OR

(b)

> The Prime Minister is very powerful.

Explain, **in detail**, why the Prime Minister is very powerful.
You should give a **maximum** of **three** reasons in your answer.

8

[Now go to question 7 starting on *Page six*]

Question 7

Study Sources 1, 2 and 3 then answer the question which follows.

SOURCE 1

Electoral reform

The debate on electoral reform of the House of Commons has been ongoing for a number of years. In May 2011, the British public were asked to vote in a referendum on replacing the current system, first-past-the-post (FPTP), with a form of proportional representation (PR) called the Alternative Vote.

More recently, Green MP Caroline Lucas proposed the Electoral Reform Bill as a Private Members' Bill. The Bill received cross-party support from five different political parties. The rise in popularity of reform groups supporting change is evidence that the debate over electoral reform is not going to disappear, if recent activities are anything to go by.

There are two sides to the debate, with opponents of change arguing that the public want to retain the current system as they recognised that it works. Supporters of FPTP argue it is simple to use and provides stable governments as well as bringing other benefits. Furthermore, the desire for change is not fully supported by the current government or the Opposition party in the House of Commons.

If the critics of FPTP are to be believed, voters are unhappy with the current system. If this is the case, why did the 2017 General Election see the highest turnout figures for 20 years?

SOURCE 2

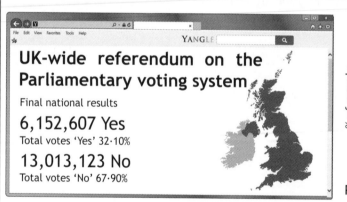

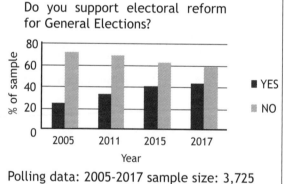

Do you support electoral reform for General Elections?

Polling data: 2005-2017 sample size: 3,725

SOURCE 3

Daily Reporter

MPs have today rejected the Private Members' Bill proposed by Green MP Caroline Lucas. If passed, the Bill would have seen a change in the voting system used in the House of Commons to a form of proportional representation. The Bill had originally received cross-party support but it was voted down by 81 to 74 votes. A disappointed Lucas commented that she would continue fighting for reform and argued that "the movement for a fairer voting system is stronger than ever – with support from across the Labour Party, UKIP, the SNP, the Lib Dems, Greens and people across the country".

MARKS

Question 7 (continued)

SOURCE 3 (continued)

Have Your Say

Molly Miller, Pro-reform supporter
4 days ago
There is a growing tide of support for changing the way we elect MPs in the House of Commons.

Electoral Reform Society
5 days ago
Our organisation has supported the idea of changing the system used for voting since 1884; we now need to act.

Joe Charlton, Opponent of reform
5 days ago
We have already had a referendum that delivered a decisive decision on reform; the government is right not to support any change to the current system.

Wes Streeting, Labour MP
1 week ago
While my party has not made a collective decision on changing to PR, I believe our electoral system is broken and that is why I support Caroline Lucas' Private Members' Bill.

Owen Winter, Founder of 'Make Votes Matter'
2 weeks ago
A change to our voting system is required. We need an electoral system that is suited to the 21st century.

Niamh Armour, Anti-reform supporter
2 months ago
If we move to a system of PR then extremist parties will gain power; our democracy cannot allow this to happen.

Iain Thorpe, Earth News
2 months ago
Our fight is not over — we will continue to campaign against the use of first-past-the-post in UK elections. We will work with a cross-party group of MPs who support our call for immediate action.

Using Sources 1, 2 and 3, give reasons to **support** and **oppose** the view of Archie Murray.

> There is widespread support for replacing the current system used to elect MPs with a form of proportional representation (PR) in the House of Commons.
>
> **View of Archie Murray**

In your answer you **must**:

- give evidence from the sources that supports Archie Murray's view

and

- give evidence from the sources that opposes Archie Murray's view

Your answer **must** be based on all **three** sources.

10

NOW GO TO SECTION 2 ON *Page eight*

SECTION 2 — SOCIAL ISSUES IN THE UNITED KINGDOM — 26 marks

MARKS

Attempt **EITHER** Part C **AND** question 14 **OR** Part D **AND** question 14

Part C	Social inequality	Page 8
Part D	Crime and the law	Page 9
Question 14		Pages 10–11

PART C — SOCIAL INEQUALITY

In your answers to questions 8, 9 and 10 you should give recent examples from the United Kingdom.

Question 8

> The private and voluntary sectors try to reduce inequalities.

Select **one** of the options below:

- Private sector
- Voluntary sector.

Describe, **in detail**, **two** ways the option you have selected tries to reduce inequalities.

4

Question 9

> Social and economic inequality continues to exist in Scotland and the UK.

Explain, **in detail**, **two** reasons why social and economic inequality continues to exist in Scotland and the UK.

6

Question 10

> Social and economic inequality has a negative consequence on families.

Explain, **in detail**, **two** reasons why social and economic inequality has a negative consequence on families.

6

[Now go to question 14 starting on *Page ten*]

MARKS

PART D — CRIME AND THE LAW

In your answers to questions 11, 12 and 13 you should give recent examples from the United Kingdom.

Question 11

There are many consequences of crime for the perpetrators.

Describe, **in detail**, **two** consequences of crime for the perpetrators.   4

Question 12

Some people commit crime as a result of economic issues.

Explain, **in detail**, **two** reasons why some people commit crime as a result of economic issues.   6

Question 13

Prisons are an effective punishment.

Explain, **in detail**, **two** reasons why prisons are an effective punishment.   6

[Now go to question 14 starting on *Page ten*]

Question 14

Study Sources 1, 2 and 3, then answer the question which follows.

You are an advisor to the Scottish Government. You have been asked to recommend **whether** the Scottish Government should build a prison for elderly prisoners **or** if they should adapt existing prisons for elderly prisoners.

Option 1	Option 2
The Scottish Government should build a prison for elderly prisoners.	The Scottish Government should adapt existing prisons for elderly prisoners.

SOURCE 1

Fact file about elderly prisoners

The prison population is ageing. People over 65 are the fastest growing age group in custody.

In March 2017 there were 102 prisoners aged over 80 in Scotland, and 5 who were 90 or older. These types of prisoners have needs that are constantly changing and a purpose-built prison would help to meet their needs. Recently there has been increasing evidence that the physical needs of elderly prisoners are not being met in current prisons, as the buildings are not suitable.

The Scottish Prison Service (SPS) has 13 publicly managed prisons and 2 privately run prisons. There have been some changes made to these buildings to cater for elderly prisoners and this has made life easier for some.

Most prisons are designed for the young and able. In the UK, there is only one prison that has a wing specifically designed for the elderly. Most prison buildings are multi-storey with only stairs and no lifts. Many have narrow doors and corridors. The conditions the prisoners have to live in make for a particularly intimidating and inaccessible environment for elderly prisoners. Prisons now have more elderly inmates with disabilities such as dementia or mobility problems, including some who are in wheelchairs. Other prisoners have incontinence issues.

One prison has tried to accommodate these prisoners; they have put in a stairlift and adapted 10 of their cells to meet elderly people's needs. This cost the Government £560,000 but has made a massive difference to elderly prisoners' lives.

SOURCE 2

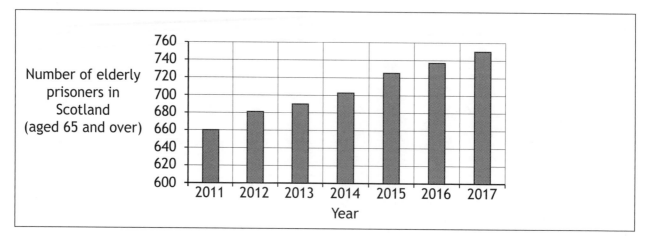

Number of elderly prisoners in Scotland (aged 65 and over) by Year

Question 14 (continued)   MARKS

SOURCE 2 (continued)

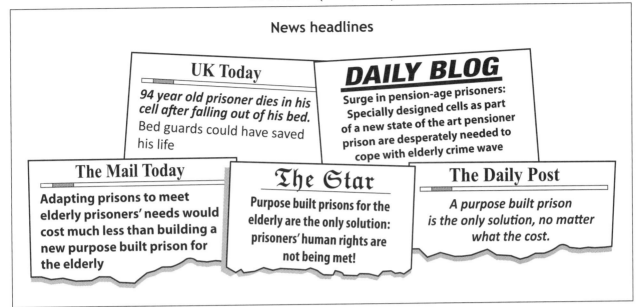

News headlines

UK Today
94 year old prisoner dies in his cell after falling out of his bed. Bed guards could have saved his life

DAILY BLOG
Surge in pension-age prisoners: Specially designed cells as part of a new state of the art pensioner prison are desperately needed to cope with elderly crime wave

The Mail Today
Adapting prisons to meet elderly prisoners' needs would cost much less than building a new purpose built prison for the elderly

The Star
Purpose built prisons for the elderly are the only solution: prisoners' human rights are not being met!

The Daily Post
A purpose built prison is the only solution, no matter what the cost.

SOURCE 3

Scotland's Inspector of Prisons

A purpose-built prison is the only solution to the constantly increasing number of elderly prisoners. This is likely to be more of a challenge in the future as prison numbers are increasing and our prisons are already overcrowded. Frail and ill, older prisoners are being denied their human rights. They often struggle to carry out the most basic daily tasks, such as carrying their meals back to their cells, and washing themselves. Adapting current prisons is not an option as the buildings are not wheelchair friendly and so many structural changes would need to take place. This would be very costly.

Government economic advisor

The Government does not have the funding to build new purpose-built prisons for the elderly. The average cost of building a new prison is £250 million and it would cost even more with the specialist equipment that would be required for a prison to cope with elderly prisoners' needs. Adapting prisons is a much more economical solution to the problem. Even basic building changes, such as installing a stairlift, would solve many of the issues that elderly prisoners have. The average cost of installing a stairlift is £3,475. Another option is to provide funding to train and hire more specialised staff to deal with elderly prisoners. Training staff for the 15 prisons in Scotland would only cost £6·5 million.

You **must** decide which option to recommend, **either** the Scottish Government should build a prison for elderly prisoners **(option 1) or** the Scottish Government should adapt existing prisons for elderly prisoners **(option 2)**.

(i)   Using Sources 1, 2 and 3, **which option would you choose?**

(ii) Give reasons to **support** your choice.

(iii) **Explain** why you did not choose the other option.

Your answer must be based on all **three** sources.   **10**

NOW GO TO SECTION 3 ON *Page twelve*

SECTION 3 — INTERNATIONAL ISSUES — 26 marks

Attempt **EITHER** Part E **AND** question 21 **OR** Part F **AND** question 21

Part E   World powers   Page 12

Part F   World issues   Page 13

Question 21   Pages 14—15

PART E — WORLD POWERS

In your answers to questions 15, 16 and 17 you should give recent examples from a world power you have studied.

Question 15

> World powers can have an economic influence on other countries.

Describe, **in detail**, **two** ways the world power you have studied can have an economic influence on other countries.

In your answer you must state the world power you have studied.

4

Question 16

> Governments try to solve social and economic problems.

Describe, **in detail**, **two** ways the government tries to solve social and economic problems.

In your answer you must state the world power you have studied.

6

Question 17

> Some groups are under-represented in politics.

Explain, **in detail**, **two** reasons why some groups are under-represented in politics.

In your answer you must state the world power you have studied.

6

[Now go to question 21 starting on *Page fourteen*]

MARKS

PART F — WORLD ISSUES

In your answers to questions 18, 19 and 20 you should give recent examples from a world issue you have studied.

Question 18

> International conflicts and issues have many causes.

Describe, **in detail**, **two** causes of an international conflict or issue you have studied.

In your answer you must state the world issue or conflict you have studied.

4

Question 19

> Organisations use many ways to try to resolve conflicts and issues across the world.

Describe, **in detail**, **two** ways in which organisations try to resolve a conflict or issue you have studied.

In your answer you must state the world issue or conflict you have studied.

6

Question 20

> Countries and their governments are often affected by conflicts and issues in other countries.

Explain, **in detail**, **two** reasons why the conflict or issue you have studied has an impact on other countries and their governments.

In your answer you must state the world issue or conflict you have studied.

6

[Now go to question 21 starting on *Page fourteen*]

Question 21

Study Sources 1, 2 and 3 then answer the question which follows.

SOURCE 1

Indonesia fact file

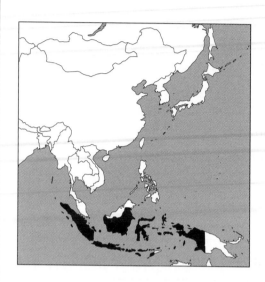

Indonesia has a population of 258 million, 87% of whom are Muslim. It is the largest island nation in the world, made up of thousands of volcanic islands. Java is the largest island with over half the population. Jakarta is the capital city with over 10 million people.

Indonesia is a member of several alliances. It is a founding member of the Association of Southeast Asian Nations [ASEAN].

It is also a member of the UN and was asked to join the G20 [group of 19 top economies plus the EU] in 2008.

Indonesia's military spending is 116th in the world. The UN officially recognises 193 countries globally.

SOURCE 2

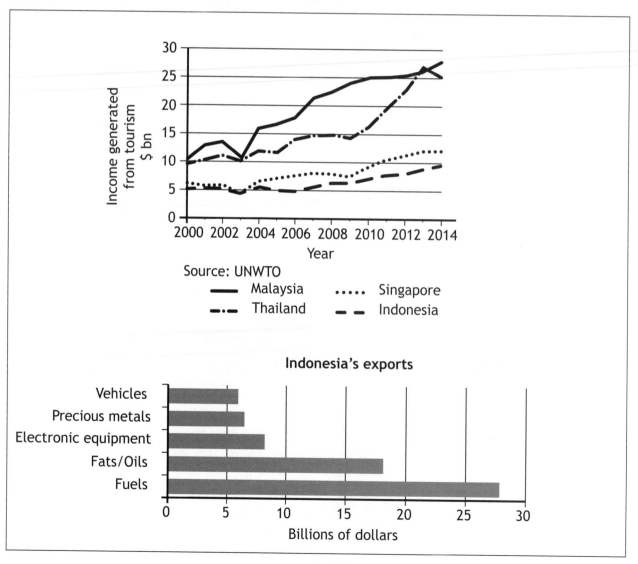

Source: UNWTO

—— Malaysia ····· Singapore
—·— Thailand — — Indonesia

Indonesia's exports

Question 21 (continued)   MARKS

SOURCE 2 (continued)

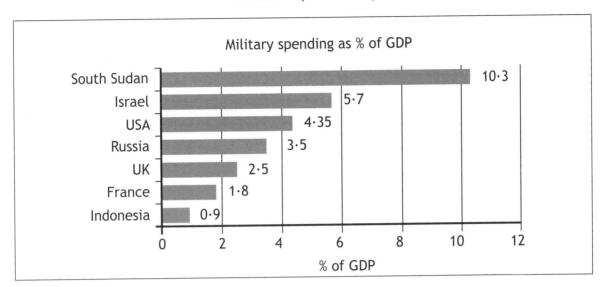

SOURCE 3

Indonesia today

Indonesia has rich biodiversity with lots of natural resources. It currently exports coal, palm oil and rubber to countries such as China, but relies on imports of finished goods such as smartphones and processed chemicals. Indonesia is the world's biggest producer of palm oil, farming over 6 million hectares. It exports 14·4 billion dollars' worth of palm oil while Malaysia exports 9·1 billion dollars' worth.

Indonesia is the only Asian member of the G20, and the G20 is responsible for 85% of the global economy. Indonesia is the world's largest supplier of instant noodles. Two of the world's top 500 companies are based in Indonesia.

In the past, Indonesia has experienced conflict within the country which meant that the government spent more money on policing than on the military. As a result the country had a low international ranking for military spending. This could be a problem in the future as China seeks new territory in the seas near Indonesia, and the country will have to protect itself.

Tourism is currently worth almost 10 billion dollars annually. There are currently 10 million visitors each year which the government hopes to double by 2020. There is now a government department to promote tourism.

Using Sources 1, 2 and 3, what **conclusions** can be drawn about the influence of Indonesia?

You should reach a conclusion about each of the following:

- The importance of the military to the Indonesian Government.
- The importance of Indonesia's exports.
- Indonesia's influence within alliances.
- The importance of tourism to Indonesia.

Your conclusions must be supported by evidence from the sources. You should link information within and between the sources in support of your conclusions.

Your answer **must** be based on all **three** sources.   **10**

[END OF QUESTION PAPER]

[BLANK PAGE]

DO NOT WRITE ON THIS PAGE

NATIONAL 5

2019

National Qualifications 2019

X849/75/11

Modern Studies

WEDNESDAY, 1 MAY
1:00 PM – 3:20 PM

Total marks — 80

SECTION 1 — DEMOCRACY IN SCOTLAND AND THE UNITED KINGDOM — 26 marks

Attempt **EITHER** Part A **AND** Question 7 **OR** Part B **AND** Question 7

Part A   Democracy in Scotland   Page 2

Part B   Democracy in the United Kingdom   Page 3

Question 7   Pages 4–5

SECTION 2 — SOCIAL ISSUES IN THE UNITED KINGDOM — 28 marks

Attempt **EITHER** Part C **AND** Question 14 **OR** Part D **AND** Question 14

Part C   Social inequality   Pages 6–7

Part D   Crime and the law   Pages 8–9

Question 14   Pages 10–11

SECTION 3 — INTERNATIONAL ISSUES — 26 marks

Attempt **EITHER** Part E **AND** Question 21 **OR** Part F **AND** Question 21

Part E   World powers   Page 12

Part F   World issues   Page 13

Question 21   Pages 14–16

Write your answers clearly in the answer booklet provided. In the answer booklet you must clearly identify the question number you are attempting.

Use **blue** or **black** ink.

Before leaving the examination room you must give your answer booklet to the Invigilator; if you do not, you may lose all the marks for this paper.

SECTION 1 — DEMOCRACY IN SCOTLAND AND THE UNITED KINGDOM — 26 marks

Attempt **EITHER** Part A **AND** Question 7 **OR** Part B **AND** Question 7

Part A   Democracy in Scotland   Page 2

Part B   Democracy in the United Kingdom   Page 3

Question 7   Pages 4—5

PART A — DEMOCRACY IN SCOTLAND

In your answers to Questions 1, 2 and 3 you should give recent examples from Scotland.

Question 1

> The Scottish Parliament has responsibility for devolved matters.

Describe, **in detail**, **two** devolved matters the Scottish Parliament has responsibility for.

4

Question 2

> Individuals have rights in a democracy.

Describe, **in detail**, **two** rights individuals have in a democracy.

6

Question 3

> Political parties use the media during election campaigns in Scotland.

Explain, **in detail**, **two** reasons why political parties use the media during election campaigns in Scotland.

6

[Now go to Question 7 starting on *Page four*]

MARKS

PART B — DEMOCRACY IN THE UNITED KINGDOM

In your answers to Questions 4, 5 and 6 you should give recent examples from the United Kingdom.

Question 4

The UK Parliament has responsibility for reserved matters.

Describe, **in detail**, **two** reserved matters the UK Parliament has responsibility for.   **4**

Question 5

Individuals have rights in a democracy.

Describe, **in detail**, **two** rights individuals have in a democracy.   **6**

Question 6

Political parties use the media during election campaigns in the UK.

Explain, **in detail**, **two** reasons why political parties use the media during election campaigns in the UK.   **6**

[Now go to Question 7 starting on *Page four*]

Question 7

Study Sources 1, 2 and 3 and then answer the question which follows.

SOURCE 1

Focus on trade unions in the United Kingdom

A trade union is an organisation which represents the interests of workers or employees. Trade unions find solutions to help workers by working together collectively. Trade union membership was once as high as 13·2 million in the late 1970s. However, currently just under 25% of all workers in the UK belong to a trade union. This is similar to the EU average membership rate of 23%. In Scotland, trade union membership is close to 30%.

Trade unions represent workers in both the private and public sectors of employment, although workers in the public sector are more likely to be a member of a trade union. The biggest public sector trade union is called Unison and it currently has over 1·3 million members, 80% of whom are female. Workers who are over 50 years old and women are far more likely to belong to a trade union than younger workers or men. In 2018, 40% of trade union members were aged over 50.

Professional employees, with degree qualifications, are also more likely to be members of a trade union than those workers employed in unskilled work with no or few qualifications.

Many workers join a trade union because they want the legal protection of the union and the numerous benefits that come along with being a member of a large organised group.

Trade unions are generally accepted as being good for democracy although some employers do not recognise them when negotiating pay and conditions of service.

SOURCE 2

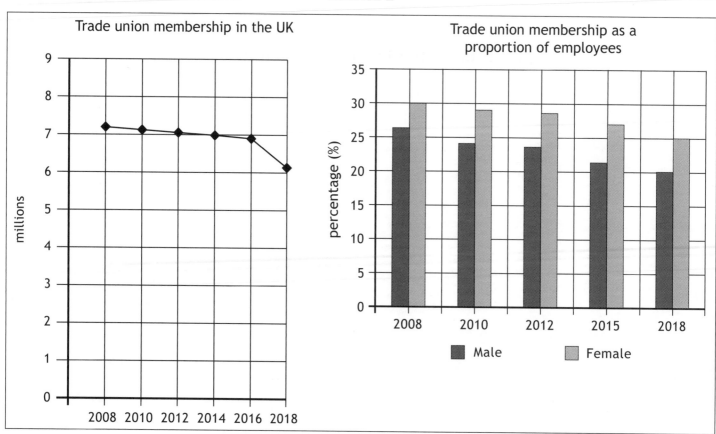

MARKS

Question 7 (continued)

SOURCE 3

Proportion of employees in a trade union in selected countries (%)			
Cyprus	55%	Italy	35%
Estonia	10%	Lithuania	8%
Finland	74%	Netherlands	20%
France	8%	Poland	12%
Germany	18%	Sweden	70%

Trade union membership as a proportion of employees

Northern Ireland

Wales

England

> >30%

25% to 30%

<25%

Using Sources 1, 2 and 3, what **conclusions** can be drawn about trade unions in the UK?

You should reach a conclusion about each of the following

- the trends in UK trade union membership

- the rate of UK trade union membership compared to European countries

- gender composition of trade union membership in the UK

- the difference in trade union membership between Scotland and England.

Your conclusions must be supported by evidence from the sources. You should link information within and between the sources in support of your conclusions.

Your answer **must** be based on all **three** sources.

10

NOW GO TO SECTION 2 ON *Page six*

SECTION 2 — SOCIAL ISSUES IN THE UNITED KINGDOM — 28 marks

Attempt **EITHER** Part C **AND** Question 14 **OR** Part D **AND** Question 14

Part C　　Social inequality　　　　　　　　　Pages 6—7

Part D　　Crime and the law　　　　　　　　Pages 8—9

Question 14　　　　　　　　　　　　　　　Pages 10—11

PART C — SOCIAL INEQUALITY

In your answers to Questions 8, 9 and 10 you should give recent examples from the United Kingdom.

Question 8

> There are several consequences of inequality on communities.

Describe, **in detail**, **two** consequences social and economic inequality can have on communities.

4

Question 9

> Inequality is a problem in Scotland and the UK.

Describe, **in detail**, **two** ways that highlight that inequality in Scotland and/or the UK is a problem.

6

Attempt **EITHER** Question 10(a) **OR** 10(b) on *Page seven*

MARKS

Attempt **EITHER** Question 10(a) **OR** 10(b)

Question 10

(a)

> The private sector has a role to play in tackling social and economic inequality.

Explain, **in detail**, why the private sector has been successful in tackling social and economic inequality.

You should give a **maximum** of **three** reasons in your answer.   **8**

OR

(b)

> Discrimination is one cause of social and economic inequality.

Explain, **in detail**, why discrimination can cause social and economic inequality for a group you have studied.

You should give a **maximum** of **three** reasons in your answer.   **8**

[Now go to Question 14 starting on *Page ten*]

MARKS

PART D — CRIME AND THE LAW

In your answers to Questions 11, 12 and 13 you should give recent examples from the United Kingdom.

Question 11

> Biological factors can cause crime.

Describe, **in detail**, **two** biological factors that can cause crime.

4

Question 12

> Crime is a problem in Scotland and the UK.

Describe, **in detail**, **two** ways that highlight that crime in Scotland and/or the UK is a problem.

6

Attempt **EITHER** Question 13(a) **OR** 13(b) on *Page nine*

MARKS

Attempt **EITHER** Question 13(a) **OR** 13(b)

Question 13

(a)

The criminal courts in Scotland are effective in tackling crime.

Explain, **in detail**, why the criminal courts in Scotland are effective in tackling crime.

You should give a **maximum** of **three** reasons in your answer.　　8

OR

(b)

The government's responses to tackling crime are ineffective.

Explain, **in detail**, why the government's responses to tackling crime have been ineffective.

You should give a **maximum** of **three** reasons in your answer.　　8

[Now go to Question 14 starting on *Page ten*]

Question 14

Study Sources 1, 2 and 3 and then answer the question which follows.

SOURCE 1

Extract from newspaper article

Can more be done to reduce reoffending?

Prisoners released in Scotland in 2017 — 678. The reoffending rate is currently 28%.

Are prisoners getting the same support and opportunities on their release?

Prisoners in Scotland are very vulnerable after release. It is often luck that determines whether they can turn their life around or not. Some prisoners on release are receiving limited support and are struggling with problems, such as no accommodation and a lack of skills and resources to start again. Some prisoners have even been handed tents on leaving prison to use as their accommodation. This can then lead to reoffending (committing further offences), in order to survive.

Charities are available to offer support for released prisoners, however they rely on the prisoners contacting them directly. This can be difficult as many prisoners do not have access to mobile phones or the internet on their release.

If used, the charities which offer support for released prisoners have excellent success rates at reducing reoffending. They can provide advice and support as to how to access state benefits and also support ex-prisoners back into education and training, giving them a better chance at staying on the straight and narrow.

However, an issue with these support services provided by charities and the voluntary sector is that they rely on funding from the public.

SOURCE 2

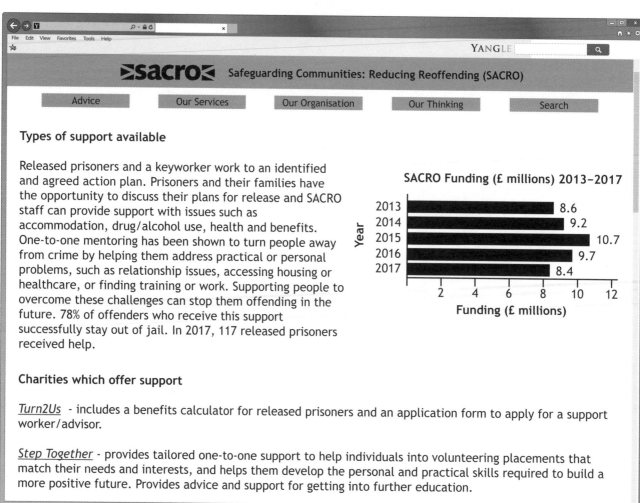

Types of support available

Released prisoners and a keyworker work to an identified and agreed action plan. Prisoners and their families have the opportunity to discuss their plans for release and SACRO staff can provide support with issues such as accommodation, drug/alcohol use, health and benefits. One-to-one mentoring has been shown to turn people away from crime by helping them address practical or personal problems, such as relationship issues, accessing housing or healthcare, or finding training or work. Supporting people to overcome these challenges can stop them offending in the future. 78% of offenders who receive this support successfully stay out of jail. In 2017, 117 released prisoners received help.

SACRO Funding (£ millions) 2013–2017

Year	Funding
2013	8.6
2014	9.2
2015	10.7
2016	9.7
2017	8.4

Funding (£ millions)

Charities which offer support

Turn2Us - includes a benefits calculator for released prisoners and an application form to apply for a support worker/advisor.

Step Together - provides tailored one-to-one support to help individuals into volunteering placements that match their needs and interests, and helps them develop the personal and practical skills required to build a more positive future. Provides advice and support for getting into further education.

MARKS

Question 14 (continued)

SOURCE 3

Released prisoner profiles

Lauren Hutt

Lauren was put in prison for three years for serious assault after getting into a fight when she was 21 years old as a result of too much alcohol. She did not get into any trouble in prison and served her full sentence. On release she was initially living with her parents until she was placed in a one-bedroom flat by her local council. Lauren contacted a charity for some support on her release. *Turn2Us* is a charity which helps prisoners turn away from crime after release. They arranged a local advisor to meet with Lauren and create an action plan for her first few months after release. This ensured she knew what she was entitled to financially and supported her on her return to a local college. Lauren has had a successful return to society and has not reoffended in the first five years since her release. This is due to her success at accessing available support.

Hamish Sinclair

Hamish was heavily involved in gangs and drugs throughout his teenage years. His relationship with his foster family broke down as a result of this and he ended up living on the streets. He was sentenced to four years in prison at the age of 17 for attempting to rob a local petrol station with a knife. While in prison Hamish battled with mental health issues and struggled to interact with other prisoners. On his release Hamish was placed in a temporary bed and breakfast for the first two weeks and was advised to contact *Step Together*, however he had no access to the internet to do so. He has since had no support for his mental health issues and is back in contact with some of the members of his old gang. He has started taking drugs again. In order to feed his habit, he began shoplifting and was arrested.

Using Sources 1, 2 and 3, give reasons to **support** and **oppose** the view of Ivy Jackson.

Enough support is being provided to reduce reoffending.

View of Ivy Jackson

In your answer you **must**

- give evidence from the sources that supports Ivy Jackson's view

and

- give evidence from the sources that opposes Ivy Jackson's view.

Your answer **must** be based on all **three** sources.

10

NOW GO TO SECTION 3 ON *Page twelve*

SECTION 3 — INTERNATIONAL ISSUES — 26 marks

Attempt **EITHER** Part E **AND** Question 21 **OR** Part F **AND** Question 21

Part E   World powers   Page 12

Part F   World issues   Page 13

Question 21   Pages 14—16

PART E — WORLD POWERS

In your answers to Questions 15, 16 and 17 you should give recent examples from a world power you have studied.

Question 15

> World powers can have a military influence on other countries.

Describe, **in detail**, **two** ways the world power you have studied can have a military influence on other countries.

In your answer you must state the world power you have studied.

4

Question 16

> Social and economic issues are experienced by some people.

Explain, **in detail**, **two** reasons why some people experience social and economic issues.

In your answer you must state the world power you have studied.

6

Question 17

> Some groups are more likely to participate in politics than others.

Explain, **in detail**, **two** reasons why some groups are more likely to participate in politics than others.

In your answer you must state the world power you have studied.

6

[Now go to Question 21 starting on *Page fourteen*]

MARKS

PART F — WORLD ISSUES

In your answers to Questions 18, 19 and 20 you should give recent examples from a world issue you have studied.

Question 18

> International conflicts and issues have an impact on people directly involved.

Describe, **in detail**, **two** ways an international conflict or issue that you have studied has an impact on people directly involved.

In your answer you must state the world issue or conflict you have studied.

4

Question 19

> International organisations have been successful in tackling many international conflicts and issues.

Explain, **in detail**, **two** reasons why attempts by international organisations to tackle the conflict or issue you have studied have been successful.

In your answer you must state the world issue or conflict you have studied.

6

Question 20

> There are many political causes of international conflicts or issues.

Explain, **in detail**, **two** political causes of an international conflict or issue you have studied.

In your answer you should state the world issue or conflict you have studied.

6

[Now go to Question 21 starting on *Page fourteen*]

Question 21

Study Sources 1, 2 and 3 and then answer the question which follows.

International Emergency Relief (IER) is about to elect a new Executive Leader. You are a member of this non-governmental organisation (NGO) and will vote to decide who should be the next leader of IER. There are two candidates, Option 1 or Option 2.

Option 1	Option 2
James Peddie	Elizabeth Sharp

SOURCE 1

James Peddie

Age: 48

Former head of Belgium's Department for Foreign Aid and Ambassador for IER in Europe

The IER is a vital international organisation that is in need of an experienced and knowledgeable leader.

As Executive Leader of IER my priorities would be:

Women's rights:

Ensuring women have equal access to all areas of life and work across the globe. To ensure countries across the world commit to this and take positive action by 2025.

Under-development in Africa:

IER have a responsibility to not just meet short-term issues within these countries but to also ensure the long-term development of these countries.

Other aims:

I believe that we need to show where all funding comes from and how the money is spent.

There is also a huge need to modernise the organisation to use modern technology to allow specialist workers to communicate with other countries without the need to travel or take extended periods of time off.

Elizabeth Sharp

Age: 39

Chief Executive of Teck International and Ambassador for IER in Asia

My experience in business will help to ensure the operation of IER is efficient and effective worldwide.

As Executive Leader of IER my priorities would be:

Emergency relief in conflict zones:

With increasing need for emergency relief in areas where conflict has had a huge impact on the local population, this should be a priority for IER.

Climate change:

We need to work towards a world where all countries are looking to address climate change and we should be actively campaigning to ensure governments across the globe set and meet targets to reduce greenhouse emissions.

Other aims:

I also believe that we need to ensure that more workers are sent to crisis areas and use their expertise to improve the situation immediately. IER would employ these specialist workers full-time to avoid clashes with other jobs.

Question 21 (continued)

SOURCE 2

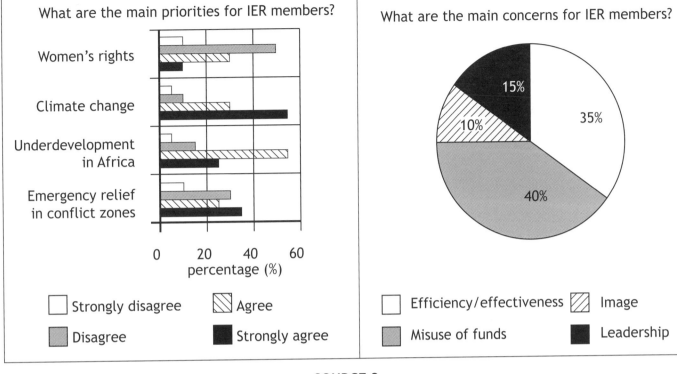

What are the main priorities for IER members?

- Women's rights
- Climate change
- Underdevelopment in Africa
- Emergency relief in conflict zones

0 20 40 60
percentage (%)

☐ Strongly disagree ▨ Agree
▨ Disagree ■ Strongly agree

What are the main concerns for IER members?

15%
35%
10%
40%

☐ Efficiency/effectiveness ▨ Image
▨ Misuse of funds ■ Leadership

SOURCE 3

Daily News

Charities under fire

A number of international NGOs have been named and shamed for not declaring how they have spent money raised and governments are calling on leaders to change practice or face penalties.

A European leader has called this a challenging time for our partners in combating world poverty.

News.org
Top priorities for world aid revealed

Our worldwide survey has identified the key areas people across the globe would like to see addressed. Over 50% of participants would like to see action taken to combat climate change and almost 50% believed that taking action on underdevelopment in Africa should be a priority for governments and NGOs.

International on Sunday
A US Senator declares NGO's as wasteful

During a recent visit to South America a US Senator criticised NGOs as being wasteful and inefficiently run, claiming that if they were run as businesses they would be more effective in delivering on their promises. This is at a time when the leaders of the G7 are about to meet and discuss this next month.

Sunday Record
The need for specialist workers in crisis zones

Many areas across the globe need access to specialist workers who have the expertise to give advice on how best to take actions to reduce the impact of man-made or natural events and to help devastated areas recover. These workers are in short supply as it is often dangerous and difficult to get time off their own work.

MARKS

Question 21 (continued)

You must decide which option to recommend, **either** James Peddie (**Option 1**) or Elizabeth Sharp (**Option 2**).

(i)   Using Sources 1, 2 and 3, **which option would you choose**?

(ii) Give reasons to **support** your choice.

(iii) **Explain** why you did not choose the other option.

Your answer must be based on all **three** sources.

10

[END OF QUESTION PAPER]

[OPEN OUT]

DO NOT WRITE ON THIS PAGE

[BLANK PAGE]

DO NOT WRITE ON THIS PAGE

NATIONAL 5

Answers

SQA NATIONAL 5
MODERN STUDIES 2019

Part A: Democracy in Scotland

1. *Candidates can be credited in a number of ways* **up to a maximum of 4 marks**.

Possible approaches to answering the question:

Political parties can campaign during a Scottish Parliament election by canvassing.
[1 mark – accurate but undeveloped point]

Political parties can campaign during a Scottish Parliament election by canvassing. Canvassing gives parties the opportunity to go door to door to speak with the public in an attempt to increase voter awareness of the party.
[2 marks – developed point]

Political parties can campaign during a Scottish Parliament election by canvassing. Canvassing gives parties the opportunity to go door to door to speak with the public in an attempt to increase voter awareness of the party. This may secure more votes for the party as the canvassers will outline and explain the party policies to be implemented once elected.
[3 marks – developed point with detail and exemplification]

Credit reference to aspects of the following:
- Use of the media – newspapers, PEBs, TV debates, social media
- Leafleting
- Posters
- Holding a public meeting/rally
- Publishing a manifesto
- Use of celebrities to gain media attention and support from voters.

Any other valid point that meets the criteria described in the general marking instructions.

2. *Candidates can be credited in a number of ways* **up to a maximum of 6 marks**.

Possible approaches to answering the question:

The Scottish Parliament has responsibility for devolved matters such as education.
[1 mark – accurate but undeveloped point]

The Scottish Parliament has responsibility for devolved matters such as education. Scottish pupils sit Nationals and Highers whereas English students sit GCSEs, AS and A-Levels.
[2 marks – developed point]

The Scottish Parliament has responsibility for devolved matters such as education. Scottish pupils sit Nationals and Highers whereas English students sit GCSEs, AS and A-Levels. In 2017 the Scottish Government introduced the revised National 5 to be examined for the first time in 2018.
[3 marks – developed point with exemplification]

Credit reference to aspects of the following:
- Health
- Local government
- Law, including most aspects of criminal and civil law, the prosecution system and the courts

- Social work
- Housing
- Tourism and economic development.

Any other valid point that meets the criteria described in the general marking instructions.

3. (a) *Candidates can be credited in a number of ways* **up to a maximum of 8 marks**.

Possible approaches to answering the question:

The Additional Member System is a more proportional system.
[1 mark – accurate but undeveloped point]

The Additional Member System is a more proportional system because the percentage of votes relates to the percentage of seats won by a party.
[2 marks – developed point]

The Additional Member System is a more proportional system because the percentage of votes relates to the percentage of seats won by a party. For example, in the 2011 election the Conservatives won about 12% of the vote and 12% of the seats.
[3 marks – developed point with exemplification]

The Additional Member System is a broadly proportional system because the percentage of votes relates to the percentage of seats won by a party. For example, in the 2011 election the Conservatives won about 12% of the vote and 12% of the seats. This can often lead to coalition governments, as no one party has a majority, which means parties work together providing better representation for voters.
[4 marks – developed point with exemplification and analysis]

Credit reference to aspects of the following:
- Retains elements of FPTP so some direct representation – voters in every constituency know who to contact
- Greater choice – each voter can contact a number of MSPs due to the regional list element
- Greater choice – two votes at the ballot box
- Smaller parties can be successful, eg Greens in Scottish Parliament.

Any other valid point that meets the criteria described in the general marking instructions.

(b) *Candidates can be credited in a number of ways* **up to a maximum of 8 marks**.

Possible approaches to answering the question:

Trade Unions

People may join a trade union to protect their rights at work.
[1 mark – accurate but undeveloped point]

People may join a trade union to protect their rights at work. For example, most secondary teachers join the EIS or SSTA.
[2 marks – accurate with exemplification]

People may join a trade union to protect their rights at work. For example, most teachers join the EIS or SSTA. They might do this because they feel that they are being asked to complete work out with their job description. The trade union will take action on their behalf eg trade unions have had discussions with the Scottish Government over unit assessments in secondary school.

[4 marks – accurate point with development and detailed exemplification]

Credit reference to aspects of the following:

Trade Unions
- Protect rights at work eg health and safety, pay, holidays, pensions
- TUs have experience negotiating with management
- TUs have legal teams you can use
- Collective action is more effective than individual action.

Pressure Groups

People may choose to join a pressure group because they are passionate about a cause.

[1 mark – accurate but undeveloped point]

People may choose to join a pressure group because they are passionate about a cause. They may choose to join Greenpeace if they are concerned about the environment.

[2 marks – developed point]

People may choose to join a pressure group because they are passionate about a cause. They may choose to join Greenpeace if they are concerned about the environment. They feel that by joining a pressure group they can have more of an impact by campaigning with other people. For example, Greenpeace has 11,000 Scottish members; this gives it strength in numbers and increases its chances of influencing the government.

[4 marks – accurate point with developed exemplification and analysis]

Credit reference to aspects of the following:

Pressure Groups
- Believe strongly about an issue such as human rights
- Collective action more effective than individual
- Media pay more attention to organised pressure groups
- Pressure groups have experience of campaigning/ protesting
- Seen as the best way to influence government in between elections.

Any other valid point that meets the criteria described in the general marking instructions.

Part B: Democracy in the United Kingdom

4. *Candidates can be credited in a number of ways up to a maximum of 4 marks.*

Possible approaches to answering the question:

Political parties can campaign during a General Election by canvassing.

[1 mark – accurate but undeveloped point]

Political parties can campaign during a General Election by canvassing. Canvassing gives parties the opportunity to go door to door to speak with the public in an attempt to increase voter awareness of the party.

[2 marks – developed point]

Political parties can campaign during a General Election by canvassing. Canvassing gives parties the opportunity to go door to door to speak with the public in an attempt to increase voter awareness of the party. This may secure more votes for the party as the canvassers will outline and explain the party policies to be implemented once elected.

[3 marks – developed point with detail and exemplification]

Credit reference to aspects of the following:
- Use of the media – newspapers, PEBS, TV debates, social media
- Leafleting
- Posters
- Holding a public meeting/rally
- Publishing a manifesto
- Use of celebrities to gain media attention and support from voters.

Any other valid point that meets the criteria described in the general marking instructions.

5. *Candidates can be credited in a number of ways up to a maximum of 6 marks.*

Possible approaches to answering the question:

The UK Parliament has responsibility for reserved matters such as immigration.

[1 mark – accurate but undeveloped point]

The UK Parliament has responsibility for reserved matters such as immigration. Every year they make a number of decisions about who has the right to visit or stay in the country.

[2 marks – developed point]

The UK Parliament has responsibility for reserved matters such as immigration. Every year they make a number of decisions about who has the right to visit or stay in the country. The UK Parliament does, however, work with the Scottish Parliament on this matter in relation to asylum seekers who are living in Scotland.

[3 marks – developed point with exemplification]

Credit reference to aspects of the following:
- Immigration
- Benefits & social security
- Defence
- Foreign policy
- Nuclear power.

Any other valid point that meets the criteria described in the general marking instructions.

6. (a) *Candidates can be credited in a number of ways up to a maximum of 8 marks.*

Possible approaches to answering the question:

One disadvantage of FPTP is that small parties are underrepresented.

[1 mark – accurate but undeveloped point]

One disadvantage of FPTP is that small parties are underrepresented. This is because the percentage of seats which a party wins in Parliament does not represent the percentage of votes they win in the election.

[2 marks – developed point]

One disadvantage of FPTP is that small parties are underrepresented. This is because the percentage of seats which a party wins in Parliament does not represent the percentage of votes they win in the election. In the 2015 General Election, UKIP got 12.6% of the votes (almost four million votes) and 1 seat.

[3 marks – developed point with exemplification]

One disadvantage of FPTP is that small parties are underrepresented because the percentage of seats which a party wins in Parliament does not represent the percentage of votes they win in the election. In the 2015 General Election, UKIP got 12.6% of the votes (almost four million votes) and 1 seat. This is unfair and is a reason why some people believe that FPTP is undemocratic and, as a result, do not vote.

> [4 marks – developed point with exemplification and analysis]

Credit reference to aspects of the following:
- If party support is spread out and not concentrated in a constituency, parties
- Will find it very difficult to get any MPs elected
- Tactical voting is possible
- There are no prizes for second place
- In safe seats parties have a great power to choose the MP
- Many won't vote for smaller parties in a safe seat
- Strong government isn't always good government
- Political parties often target marginal seats and can be seen to ignore constituencies with safe seats.

Any valid point that meets the criteria described in the general marking instructions.

(b) *Candidates can be credited in a number of ways **up to a maximum of 8 marks.***

Possible approaches to answering the question:

Trade Unions

People may join a trade union to protect their rights at work.

> [1 mark – accurate but undeveloped point]

People may join a trade union to protect their rights at work. For example, rail workers join the Rail, Maritime and Transport Union (RMT).

> [2 marks – accurate with exemplification]

People may join a trade union to protect their rights at work. For example, rail workers join the Rail, Maritime and Transport Union (RMT). The trade union will take action on their behalf eg the RMT met with Transport for London ahead of planned industrial action to try to negotiate a deal on behalf of their members and avoid further industrial action taking place.

> [4 marks – accurate point with development and detailed exemplification]

Credit reference to aspects of the following:

Trade Unions
- Protect rights at work eg health and safety, pay, holidays, pensions
- TUs have experience negotiating with management
- TUs have legal teams you can use
- Collective action is more effective than individual action.

Pressure Groups

People may choose to join a pressure group because they are passionate about a cause.

> [1 mark – accurate but undeveloped point]

People may choose to join a pressure group because they are passionate about a cause. They may choose to join Greenpeace if they are concerned about the environment.

> [2 marks – developed point]

People may choose to join a pressure group because they are passionate about a cause. They may choose to join Greenpeace if they are concerned about the environment. They feel that by joining a pressure group they can have more of an impact by campaigning with other people. For example, Greenpeace has 130,000 UK supporters; this gives it strength in numbers and increases its chances of influencing the government.

> [4 marks – accurate point with developed exemplification and analysis]

Credit reference to aspects of the following:

Pressure Groups
- Believe strongly about an issue such as human rights
- Collective action more effective than individual
- Media pay more attention to organised pressure groups
- Pressure groups have experience of campaigning/ protesting
- Seen as the best way to influence government in between elections.

Any valid point that meets the criteria described in the general marking instructions.

7. *Candidates can be credited in a number of ways **up to a maximum of 10 marks.***

Possible approaches to answering the question:

Evidence to support Morag's view that the House of Lords does need further reform includes:

Source 2 highlights that less than 5% of the House of Lords has an ethnic-minority background.

> [1 mark – accurate use of source 2 but minimal development]

Source 2 highlights that less than 5% of the House of Lords has an ethnic-minority background, which is an under representation, as ethnic minorities make up 13% of the UK population.

> [2 marks – accurate use of source 2 with analysis]

Source 2 highlights that the percentage of House of Lords under 60 has decreased from 22% to 16% yet almost three-quarters of the population (77%) are under 60, highlighting under representation of under 60s. This is backed up by source 3 that shows that two peers are under the age of 40 but more than ten times that number are over the age of 90.

> [3 marks – accurate information from two sources with analysis]

Credit reference to aspects of the following:
- None of the 790 members are directly elected (source 1)
- Women and disabled are also under represented (source 2)
- The number of privately educated lords is 50% which is disproportionate to the UK population of 7% (source 2)
- Lord Tyler states that House of Lords was "London's best day centre for the elderly" with members able to claim up to £300 per day in expenses for just "turning up and shuffling off"

Evidence to oppose Morag's view that the House of Lords does not need further reform includes:

Source 1 highlights that many Lords bring great experience and expertise to Parliament.

> [1 mark – accurate use of source 1 but minimal development]

Source 1 highlights that many Lords bring great experience and expertise to Parliament in the field of medicine, law, business and science and this is supported by source 3 which states that the House of Lords can be useful when opposing bills in the House of Parliament.

> [2 marks – accurate use of two sources]

Source 1 highlights that many Lords bring great experience and expertise to Parliament in the field of medicine, law, business and science and this is supported by source 3 which states that the House of Lords can be useful when opposing bills in the House of Parliament. Source 3 also highlights that House of Lords can play a valuable role in scrutinising and revising legislation.

[3 marks – well developed point; accurate use of two sources]

Credit reference to aspects of the following:
- In 1995 there were 7% women in the Lords, in 2015 about 25% were women (source 2)
- Two of the Lord Speakers have been female – Baroness D'Souza & Baroness Hayman (source 1)
- Lack of enthusiasm for change from both houses as well as the British public (source 3)
- Disabled members have increased by 9% (source 2)
- In 1995 over half of the members were hereditary peers whereas today approximately 90% of members are life peers (source 1).

Any valid point that meets the criteria described in the general marking instruction.

Part C: Social Inequality

8. *Candidates can be credited in a number of ways **up to a maximum of 4 marks**.*

Possible approaches to answering the question:

The Government has tried to reduce the inequalities experienced by women/ethnic minorities/elderly by passing laws.

[1 mark – accurate but undeveloped point]

The Government has tried to reduce the inequalities faced by women by passing the Equality Act which makes it illegal to pay women less if they are doing the same job as men.

[2 marks – accurate point with development]

The Government has tried to reduce the inequalities faced by the disabled by passing laws such as the Equality Act in 2010 which makes it illegal to discriminate against a disabled person in the areas of employment and education. In the area of employment, employers cannot treat disabled people differently and must provide disabled employees with special equipment to help them do their job.

[3 marks – accurate, well developed point with exemplification]

Credit reference to aspects of the following:
- Sex Discrimination Act (Women)
- Women on Board Report (Women)
- Race Relations Act (Ethnic Minorities)
- Inclusive Communication
- Disabled people are also protected by the UN Convention on the Rights of Persons with Disabilities (CRPD)
- Office for Disability Issues
- The Equalities & Human Rights Commission
- Equality Advisory & Support Service (EASS)
- Making Sport Inclusive Programme
- Forced Marriage (Civil Protection) Act 2007 – Forced Marriage Protection Order (FMPO)
- Government Campaigns: One Scotland, Show Racism the Red Card etc.

Any other valid point that meets the criteria described in the general marking instruction.

9. *Candidates can be credited in a number of ways **up to a maximum of 6 marks**.*

Possible approaches to answering the question:

Some people have a better standard of living because they have a good job.

[1 mark – accurate but undeveloped point]

Some people have a better standard of living because they have a good job that pays well, such as a teacher.

[2 marks – accurate point with exemplification]

Some people have a better standard of living because they have a good job that pays well, such as a teacher. This may be because they have a number of qualifications, such as a degree, having gone to university for several years.

[3 marks – accurate point with development and exemplification]

Some people are economically disadvantaged because of their family structure. Single parents, for example, may find it harder to find a well-paid job. A two parent family is likely to have a much higher income. Even if a lone parent has good qualifications they can only work at certain times as their child care costs are too high. A family with two parents has a better standard of living; as a result, this may have a positive impact on the education and health of their children.

[4 marks – relevant, accurate point with development, analysis and exemplification]

Credit reference to aspects of the following:
- Employment
- Skills and experience
- Number of dependent children
- Education/training
- Poor health: unable to work due to illness
- Racial discrimination
- Gender discrimination
- Criminal record makes it difficult to find work
- Access to healthcare
- Housing/environment
- Inheritance.

Any other valid point that meets the criteria described in the general marking instructions.

10. *Candidates can be credited in a number of ways **up to a maximum of 6 marks**.*

Possible approaches to answering the question:

Ethnic minorities still face inequality in society because they still face racism in some areas of society.

[1 mark – accurate but undeveloped point]

Older people still face inequality in society because they face discrimination in the world of work because some employers think they don't have IT skills.

[2 marks – accurate with development]

Women still face inequality in society because of sexism. Employers, for example, might not want to employ a woman as they think she will need time off to look after her children. This means that women find it more difficult to find suitable work and as a result often work part-time in occupations like cleaning, childcare etc. Many women feel that the glass ceiling still exists which limits opportunities for promotion in their careers.

[4 marks – accurate point with development, analysis and exemplification]

Credit reference to aspects of the following:
- Ethnic minorities: prejudice, language barriers, poor educational attainment, higher unemployment rates, specific health issues

- Older people: ageism; financial preparation for retirement; previous occupation; family support; changes to benefit system, ie bedroom tax and employability
- Women: sexism; glass ceiling; pay gap; employment in 5Cs, child care availability and costs
- Disabled: prejudice; over qualification; lack of work experience; family support network; continuing health issues; reliance on benefits
- Lone parents: prejudice, family commitments, lack of qualifications, no support network/child care
- Unemployed: stigma of long term unemployment, lack of experience
- Changes to the benefit system/recession.

Any other valid point that meets the criteria described in the general marking instructions.

Part D: Crime and the Law

11. *Candidates can be credited in a number of ways* **up to a maximum of 4 marks.**

    Possible approaches to answering the question:

    The Scottish Government has tried to tackle crime by lowering drink-drive limits.
    [1 mark – accurate but undeveloped point]

    The Scottish Government has tried to tackle crime by making drink-drive limits clearer by reducing the maximum limit; this means that there should be fewer road traffic accidents, deaths and injuries.
    [2 marks – accurate point with development]

    The Scottish Government has tried to tackle crime by making drink-drive limits clearer by reducing the maximum limit; this means that there should be fewer road traffic accidents, deaths and injuries. People are less likely now to drink at all if driving given that the legal limit has been lowered from 80 mg to 50 mg of alcohol in every 100 ml of blood.
    [3 marks – accurate point with development and exemplification]

    Credit reference to aspects of the following:
    - Early release from prison
    - Operation Blade
    - Anti-sectarian legislation
    - Neighbourhood watch
    - CCTV
    - Speed cameras
    - Tags/alternatives to prison
    - ASBOs
    - Supervision orders/tagging orders
    - Community policing.

    Any other valid point that meets the criteria described in the general marking instructions.

12. *Candidates can be credited in a number of ways* **up to a maximum of 6 marks.**

    Possible approaches to answering the question:

    Some people are more affected by crime if they are the victim of a crime.
    [1 mark – accurate but undeveloped point]

    Some people are more affected by crime if they are the victim of a crime. Victims of assault may be fearful that it could happen and may be afraid to leave their home.
    [2 marks – accurate point with development]

Some people are more affected by crime if they are the victim of a crime. Victims of assault may be fearful that it could happen and may be afraid to leave their home. They may also have alarm systems fitted in their home, at a cost, in order to try to feel more secure.
[3 marks – accurate point with development and exemplification]

Credit reference to aspects of the following:
- Businesses – insurance premiums may rise in areas with high crime rate
- Perpetrators – loss of family, job, house should they be found guilty/given prison sentence
- Community – closure of businesses/facilities due to crime/vandalism/robbery
- Families of perpetrators – targeted by others in the community
- Some people are more vulnerable to crime – ethnic minorities, young people, elderly.

Any other valid point that meets the criteria described in the general marking instructions.

13. *Candidates can be credited in a number of ways* **up to a maximum of 6 marks.**

    Possible approaches to answering the question:

    Drug addiction can cause crime.
    [1 mark – accurate but undeveloped point]

    Drug addiction can cause crime. Drug addicts need to pay for their drugs and may steal to fund their habit.
    [2 marks – accurate point with development]

    Drug addiction can cause crime. Drug addicts need to pay for their drugs and may to steal to fund their habit and are more likely to be arrested for crimes such as burglary, shoplifting, robbery or handling stolen goods. Areas with high rates of drug problems are more likely to have high levels of crime.
    [3 marks – accurate point with development and exemplification]

    Credit reference to aspects of the following:
    - Poverty/deprivation
    - Peer pressure
    - Family influence
    - Alcohol abuse
    - Mental illness
    - Violent media images
    - Homelessness
    - Poor educational attainment
    - Social exclusion
    - Greed – white collar crime.

    Any other valid point that meets the criteria described in the general marking instructions.

14. *Candidates can be credited in a number of ways* **up to a maximum of 10 marks.**

    Possible approaches to answering the question:

    ### Option 1: Ban Legal Highs

    The Government should ban legal highs as legal highs have been linked to hospital admissions for things such as poisoning, mental health issues, and in extreme cases death.
    [1 mark – evidence drawn from source 1]

    The Government should ban legal highs as legal highs have been linked to hospital admissions for things such as poisoning, mental health issues, and in extreme cases death. This is backed up in source 2 which shows that there has been an increase in deaths as a result of legal highs.

[2 marks – evidence linked from Source 1 and Source 2]

The Government should ban legal highs as legal highs have been linked to hospital admissions for things such as poisoning, mental health issues, and in extreme cases death. This is backed up in source 2 which shows that there has been an increase in deaths as a result of legal highs. The increase in deaths has gone from just over 40 to almost 120, which is almost triple the number.

[3 marks – evidence linked from source 1 and Source 2 with evaluative comment]

Credit reference to aspects of the following:
- These drugs are often included in everyday household products and are often labelled not for human consumption (source 1).
- Mandeep Khan states that "more of my time as a paramedic is being taken up dealing with the consequences of legal highs. The misuse of these drugs diverts our attention from cases that are much more important" (source 3).

Reasons for rejecting the other option:

I rejected Option 2 as although source 2 states 66% of young people know that legal highs could result in death source 1 highlights that the UK has the most severe problem with legal highs in Western Europe, with significant numbers of young people regularly admitting to taking legal highs.

[2 marks – evidence linked from source 1 and source 2]

Option 2: Do not ban Legal Highs

The Government should not ban legal highs as there was a mass demonstration against the proposed legislation due to the inclusion of nitrous oxide, otherwise known as laughing gas, within the bill. Nitrous oxide is commonly used as anaesthetic during dentistry, childbirth and as a mood enhancer.

[1 mark – evidence drawn from source 1]

The Government should not ban legal highs as in a recent survey 53% of 16–25 year olds stated that they had never taken legal highs with a further 10% only ever having taken them once (source 2). This is supported by source 1 when it states that despite media attention around half of young people have never experimented with legal highs.

[2 marks – evidence linked from source 1 and source 2]

Credit reference to aspects of the following:
- Control and monitoring of legal highs is very difficult (source 3)
- Often new versions are created and sold just as fast as the Government can ban them (source 3)
- There has been little or no research into the long term or short term risks of taking legal highs (source 1).

Reasons for rejecting the other option:

I rejected Option 1 as although Mandeep Khan states that lots of people are unaware of the dangers of legal highs source 2 highlights that 66% of young people know that legal highs result in death.

[2 marks – evidence linked from source 2 and source 3]

Any other valid reason that meets the criteria described in the general marking instructions.

Part E: World Powers

15. *Candidates can be credited in a number of ways **up to a maximum of 4 marks**.*

Possible approaches to answering the question:

USA

In America, Barack Obama introduced a new health care law, nicknamed Obamacare.

[1 mark – accurate point]

In America, Barack Obama introduced a new health care law called the Affordable Care Act (Obamacare). The Act was designed to increase the affordability and quality of health insurance and lower the number of uninsured. This has helped many people, especially those on low incomes, younger people and ethnic minorities.

[3 marks – accurate point with development and exemplification]

Credit reference to aspects of the following:
- Medicare, Medicaid and State Children's Health Insurance Program (covers children who do not qualify for Medicaid)
- Temporary Assistance for Needy Families (TANF)
- Affirmative Action programmes as they apply today eg the Supreme Court has basically ruled that consideration of an applicant's race/ethnicity is legal
- American Recovery and Reinvestment Act 2009 – provides expansion of unemployment benefits, social welfare provision, education and health care
- No Child Left Behind (NCLB) 2001 – aimed to improve performance in public schools to improve qualifications/employability of all children. Backed with big increases in federal funding but on-going debate as to success
- Race to the Top is a $4.35 billion United States Department of Education contest created to spur innovation and reforms in state and local district education. It is funded as part of the American Recovery and Reinvestment Act of 2009
- Funded as part of the American Recovery and Reinvestment Act of 2009
- Food stamps now known as Supplemental Nutrition Assistance Programme (SNAP) to provide healthy food for poor families
- Federal minimum wage.

China

Today most farms operate as private businesses and decisions about what to produce and how to produce are made by farmers. The government created the Household Responsibility System. Farmers have to give a certain amount to the government, but any surplus is kept by the farmer. This means that poor farmers are allowed to sell their goods for a profit thus reducing inequality.

[3 marks – accurate point with development and exemplification]

Credit reference to aspects of the following:
- Dismantling of work permit system (Hukou)
- Foreign investment, encouragement of private business (Open Door Policy and Special Economic Zones)
- Encouraging rural areas and small towns to develop entrepreneurs and industrial growth (Township and Village Enterprises)
- Development of social security system
- Better rights for women
- Improving health services, housing and reducing crime.

South Africa

Credit reference to aspects of the following:
- Affirmative Action
- Black Economic Empowerment (BEE)

- Programmes to ensure everyone has access to drinkable water, sanitation and electricity
- Land redistribution policy.

Any other valid point that meets the criteria described in the general marking instruction.

16. *Candidates can be credited in a number of ways* **up to a maximum of 6 marks.**

Possible approaches to answering the question:

Citizens in the US have the right to vote for a candidate in an election.
[1 mark – accurate point]

Citizens in the US have the right to vote for a candidate in an election. In 2016, millions of people voted for Hillary Clinton in the Presidential Election.
[2 marks – accurate point with exemplification]

People in China have the right to vote in village elections. This allows citizens the opportunity to elect village committees and village leaders as a form of local democracy. The elected representatives are entrusted with managing local affairs.
[3 marks – accurate, well developed point]

Credit reference to aspects of the following:

Clear reference to specific aspects of political systems of chosen G20 country.
- Standing for election
- Voting in elections at various levels
- Participating in political parties, trade unions, pressure groups
- Free speech
- Freedom of press
- Protection by the law.

Any other valid point that meets the criteria described in the general marking instructions.

17. *Candidates can be credited in a number of ways* **up to a maximum of 6 marks.**

Possible approaches to answering the question:

The USA has the ability to influence other countries due to the size of its military.
[1 mark – undeveloped point]

The USA has the ability to influence other countries due to the size of its military. The USA military is often referred to as the 'world policeman' and has been able to influence countries such as Afghanistan and Libya.
[2 marks – accurate point with development]

Brazil has the ability to influence other countries due to the fact it is a growing economy and is a member of BRICS. Brazil is also the single biggest supplier of agricultural products to the European Union so is a crucial trading partner. Furthermore Brazil has recently been influential in the 'South-South' Cooperation, becoming a donor to developing African countries, providing $23 million dollars to Mozambique to help with the development of HIV/AIDs treatments. This cooperation is seen as being more influential than the 'tied aid' models of the past.
[4 marks – well explained point, with exemplification and analysis]

Credit reference to aspects of the following:
- Trade
- Defence
- Diplomatic support
- Ideology

- Immigration
- Culture.

Any other valid point that meets the criteria described in the general marking instructions.

18. *Candidates can be credited in a number of ways* **up to a maximum of 4 marks.**

Possible approaches to answering the question:

African Union has deployed peacekeepers in Burundi.
[1 mark – accurate point]

NATO has continued to try to bring stability in Iraq. They have recently introduced military medicine courses to train new paramedics and have provided support with the maintenance of tanks and armoured vehicles.
[2 marks – accurate point with exemplification]

Oxfam attempts to address famine in South Sudan. In 2016 Oxfam helped more than 600,000 people across the country by providing food and water. Oxfam helped to build and repair boreholes and wells, test quality levels, treat water, and train people to look after and maintain their own water supply.
[3 marks – developed point with detailed exemplification]

Credit reference to aspects of the following:
- UNICEF
- WHO
- UNESCO
- FAO
- AU ceasefire monitors in Darfur
- AU force in Somalia
- Oxfam – supporting refugees in Syria with clean drinking water, relief supplies, improving sanitation and giving information on rights
- Oxfam – Malawi food crisis – reached over 400,000 people with assistance, including cash to buy food, tools to improve crops and seeds including more resilient options to drought such as sweet potato vines.

Any other valid point that meets the criteria described in the general marking instructions.

19. *Candidates can be credited in a number of ways* **up to a maximum of 6 marks.**

Possible approaches to answering the question:

Issue – Underdevelopment in Africa

Many people in African countries do not have access to appropriate levels of healthcare.
[1 mark – accurate but undeveloped point]

Many people in African countries do not have access to appropriate levels of healthcare and as a result many people die each year from illnesses such as malaria.
[2 marks – accurate point with development]

Some poorer African countries have inadequate healthcare with too few doctors and nurses. This makes it more difficult to treat preventable illnesses such as diarrhoeal diseases. Each day over 2000 children die from diarrhoeal diseases around the world, more than AIDS, malaria and measles.
[3 marks – accurate point with development and exemplification]

Credit reference to aspects of the following:
- Unsafe water/poor sanitary conditions
- Low life expectancy/high infant mortality rates

- High illiteracy rates/low levels of education (including attendance)
- Gender inequalities
- Refugees
- Piracy
- Child soldiers
- Destroyed infrastructure
- Human rights abuses
- Effects of terrorism
- Restrictions to civil liberties.

Any other valid point that meets the criteria described in the general marking instruction.

20. *Candidates can be credited in a number of ways up to a maximum of 6 marks.*

Possible approaches to answering the question:

Some international organisations are unsuccessful at tackling international terrorism because they do not get enough help from member countries.

[1 mark – accurate but undeveloped point]

NATO's methods are unsuccessful at tackling international terrorism because although it is a very powerful military alliance, terrorists are often not easily identifiable. They are not like a country which would be easier for NATO to fight against in the traditional sense. Terrorists don't wear uniforms and don't stick to one country's borders.

[3 marks – accurate developed point with exemplification]

NATO can't support people who have come under threat from their own governments. Since 2011 it has not been able to stop the ongoing conflict between the two warring factions in Libya and as a result it has been unable to protect civilians effectively. NATO is not set up to help install new governments and ensure security and stability in places like Libya; it was only effective in the military conflict against Colonel Gaddafi. After this, NATO members did not want the expense of rebuilding the country in the long term.

[4 marks – accurate developed point with exemplification and analysis]

Credit reference to aspects of the following:
- Lack of training of local security services
- Tribal/Civil War in Africa
- Corrupt government
- Sanctions affect some countries more than others
- The extent of poverty
- Financial constraints
- Lack of cooperation
- Inappropriate aid
- Unfair trade
- Fair trade
- Increased access to anti-retroviral therapy
- Increased enrolment in education
- Success of UN Specialised Agencies
- Success of Sustainable Development Goals.

Any other valid point that meets the criteria described in the general marking instructions.

21. *Candidates can be credited in a number of ways up to a maximum of 10 marks.*

Possible approaches to answering the question:

The problem of crime in Japan compared to other countries

Conclusion: Compared to many other countries there are relatively low levels of crime in Japan.

[1 mark for a valid conclusion]

Conclusion: Compared to many other countries there are relatively low levels of crime in Japan.

Evidence: Japan had 22 crimes per 1000 people in 2014 (source 1), which is only about one quarter of the EU figure of 80 and lower than all the countries mentioned (source 2).

[3 marks – valid conclusion with evidence from two sources and evaluative terminology]

The effects of the changing population structure in Japan

Conclusion: As the elderly population increases so do social and economic problems in Japan.

[1 mark for a valid conclusion]

Conclusion: As the elderly population increases so do social and economic problems in Japan.

Evidence: Source 1 highlights that increased poverty and a different population structure will make old age pensions and elderly care very expensive in the future. As source 2 shows the elderly population will almost double in 40 years but those paying tax (15–64 years) will fall to just over 50% of the population.

[3 marks for a valid conclusion with supporting evidence and evaluative terminology]

Also credit reference to:
- Housing is getting expensive as a result of the aging population (source 3); 61% own their home, lower than the EU, France, Italy and Argentina
- Japan has a high life expectancy (source 3) but this will be difficult to maintain as fewer will be paying tax (source 3)
- A growing elderly population is listed as one of Japan's problems (source 1).

The effect of poverty on working age women

Conclusion: Poverty decreases the happiness level of working age women.

[1 mark for a valid conclusion]

Conclusion: Poverty decreases the happiness level of working age women.

Evidence: Source 1 highlights that one third of working age women now live in poverty with part time work preventing women from having financial savings; this is a massive worry for Japanese women. This is supported by source 3 which highlights that the average happiness level for women is 4.67 (out of 10) but for working age women it is only 3.2 which is almost half of the average happiness level for men.

[3 marks for valid conclusion with supporting evidence and evaluation]

The country most like Japan

Conclusion: South Korea is most like Japan.

[1 mark for a valid conclusion]

Conclusion: South Korea is most like Japan.

Evidence: In South Korea the poverty rate is 16.5% and in Japan it is 16% (sources 1 and 2).

[2 marks for a valid conclusion with supporting evidence]

Conclusion: South Korea is most like Japan.

Evidence: In South Korea only 0·5% more people in poverty; this is the closest to Japan at 16% with crime rate in South Korea also being closest to that of Japan – 22 per 1000 in Japan and 32 per 1000 in South Korea.

[3 marks for valid conclusion with supporting evidence and evaluation]

Also credit reference to:
• Internet users – 865 per 1000 in Japan and South Korea – highest of all the countries mentioned (sources 1 and 3).

Any other valid point that meets the criteria described in the general marking instructions.

NATIONAL 5 MODERN STUDIES 2018

Part A: Democracy in Scotland

1. *Candidates can be credited in a number of ways up to a maximum of 4 marks.*

Possible approaches to answering the question:

MSPs can represent their constituents in the Scottish Parliament by asking a question at First Minister's Question Time.

[1 mark – accurate but undeveloped point]

MSPs can represent their constituents in the Scottish Parliament by asking a question at First Minister's Question Time. FMQT takes place every Thursday at midday.

[2 marks – accurate point with development]

MSPs can represent their constituents in the Scottish Parliament by asking a question at First Minister's Question Time. FMQT takes place every Thursday at midday. Recently, Conservative MSP Liz Smith asked the First Minister whether the Scottish Government will review the school inspection process.

[3 marks – accurate point with development and exemplification]

Credit reference to aspects of the following:
• taking part in a debate in the Scottish Parliament
• proposing a Members' Bill in the Parliament
• voting on new or changes to existing laws
• working/membership of a committee
• asking a question at General Question Time.

2. *Candidates can be credited in a number of ways up to a maximum of 6 marks.*

Possible approaches to answering the question:

Pressure Groups

One method used by pressure groups to gain influence in a democracy is to organise a petition.

[1 mark – accurate but undeveloped point]

One method used by pressure groups to gain influence in a democracy is to organise a petition. Recently many petitions have been submitted to the Scottish Parliament Petitions Committee.

[2 marks – accurate point with development]

One method used by pressure groups to gain influence in a democracy is to organise a petition. Recently many petitions have been submitted to the Scottish Parliament Petitions Committee. For example, Fans Against Criminalisation submitted a petition with nearly 10,000 signatures calling for the repeal of the Offensive Behaviour Act.

[3 marks – accurate point with development and exemplification]

Credit reference to aspects of the following:
• organise a protest/demonstration
• lobby a representative such as an MP, MSP or Councillor
• leaflet/poster campaigns
• take 'direct action'
• organise a social media campaign.

Possible approaches to answering the question:

Trade Unions

One method used by trade unions to gain influence in a democracy is to organise a demonstration.

[1 mark – accurate but undeveloped point]

One method used by trade unions to gain influence in a democracy is to organise a demonstration. Trade unions often organise demonstrations to draw the government's attention to their members' concerns.

[2 marks – accurate point with development]

One method used by trade unions to gain influence in a democracy is to organise a demonstration. Trade unions often organise demonstrations to draw the government's attention to their members' concerns. For example, the UNITE union organised a national demonstration in March 2017 to highlight their concerns for the NHS using the slogan 'Our NHS, no cuts, no closures, no privatisation'.

[3 marks – accurate point with development and exemplification]

Credit reference to aspects of the following:
• lobbying a representative such as an MP, MSP or Councillor
• leaflet/poster campaigns
• taking industrial action eg work-to-rule/overtime ban/ strike
• organising a social media campaign
• negotiations with employer.

3. (a) *Candidates can be credited in a number of ways up to a maximum of 8 marks.*

Possible approaches to answering the question:

People choose not to vote because they don't identify with one of the main political parties.

[1 mark – accurate but undeveloped point]

People choose not to vote because they don't identify with one of the main political parties. They view the party policies as being very similar eg in 2017 both Labour and Conservative pledged to build one million homes.

[3 marks – accurate point with development and exemplification]

People choose not to vote because they don't identify with one of the main political parties. They view the party policies as being very similar eg in 2017 both Labour and Conservative pledged to build one million homes. This may have contributed to around one in three people choosing not to vote.

[4 marks – accurate point with development, exemplification and analysis]

Credit reference to aspects of the following:
• basic right not to vote
• voter apathy
• have not registered
• safe seats
• lack of trust in MSPs/political system

- lack of role models
- alternative outlets for participation eg pressure groups.

(b) *Candidates can be credited in a number of ways up to a maximum of 8 marks.*

Possible approaches to answering the question:

The First Minister is very powerful because they are the leader of the largest party in the Scottish Parliament.
[1 mark – accurate but undeveloped point]

The First Minister is very powerful because they are the leader of the largest party in the Scottish Parliament.

In 2016, Nicola Sturgeon was returned as First Minister with 63 MSPs.
[2 marks – accurate point with development]

The First Minister is very powerful because they are the leader of the largest party in the Scottish Parliament.

In 2016, Nicola Sturgeon was returned as First Minister with 63 MSPs. This was more than any other party and allows the First Minister to implement government legislation eg the Budget.
[4 marks – accurate point with development, exemplification and analysis]

Credit reference to aspects of the following:
- power of appointment – hiring and firing ministers
- Executive head
- chairing the Cabinet and setting the Cabinet agenda
- media attention
- relationships with foreign leaders.

Part B: Democracy in the United Kingdom

4. *Candidates can be credited in a number of ways up to a maximum of 4 marks.*

Possible approaches to answering the question:

MPs can represent their constituents in the UK Parliament by asking a question at Prime Minister's Question Time.
[1 mark – accurate but undeveloped point]

MPs can represent their constituents in the UK Parliament by asking a question at Prime Minister's Question Time. PMQT takes place every Wednesday at midday.
[2 marks – accurate point with development]

MPs can represent their constituents in the UK Parliament by asking a question at Prime Minister's Question Time. PMQT takes place every Wednesday at midday. Recently, SNP MP Alison Thewliss asked a question around personal independence payments.
[3 marks – accurate point with development and exemplification]

Credit reference to aspects of the following:
- taking part in a debate in the House of Commons
- proposing a Private Members' Bill within the Commons
- voting on new or changes to existing laws
- working/membership of a Select Committee
- asking a question at Question Time.

5. *Candidates can be credited in a number of ways up to a maximum of 6 marks.*

Possible approaches to answering the question:

Pressure Groups

One method used by pressure groups to gain influence in a democracy is to organise a petition.
[1 mark – accurate but undeveloped point]

One method used by pressure groups to gain influence in a democracy is to organise a petition. Recently many petitions have been organised online using sites such as 'change.org'.
[2 marks – accurate point with development]

One method used by pressure groups to gain influence in a democracy is to organise a petition. If a petition obtains more than 100,000 signatures, then the government is obliged to consider debating the issue in the House of Commons, such as the debate held over President Trump's state visit to the UK which received 1·5 million signatures.
[3 marks – accurate point with development and exemplification]

Credit reference to aspects of the following:
- organise a protest/demonstration
- lobby a representative such as an MP, MSP or Councillor
- leaflet/poster campaigns
- take 'direct action'
- organise a social media campaign.

Possible approaches to answering the question:

Trade Unions

One method used by trade unions to gain influence in a democracy is to organise a demonstration.
[1 mark – accurate but undeveloped point]

One method used by trade unions to gain influence in a democracy is to organise a demonstration. Trade unions often organise demonstrations to draw the government's attention to their members' concerns.
[2 marks – accurate point with development]

One method used by trade unions to gain influence in a democracy is to organise a demonstration. Trade unions often organise demonstrations to draw the government's attention to their members' concerns. For example, the UNITE union organised a national demonstration in March 2017 to highlight their concerns for the NHS using the slogan 'Our NHS, no cuts, no closures, no privatisation'.
[3 marks – accurate point with development and exemplification]

Credit reference to aspects of the following:
- lobbying a representative such as an MP, MSP or Councillor
- leaflet/poster campaigns
- taking industrial action eg work-to-rule/overtime ban/strike
- organising a social media campaign
- negotiations with employer.

6. **(a)** *Candidates can be credited in a number of ways up to a maximum of 8 marks.*

Possible approaches to answering the question:

People choose not to vote because they don't identify with one of the main political parties.
[1 mark – accurate but undeveloped point]

People choose not to vote because they don't identify with one of the main political parties. They view the party policies as being very similar eg in 2017 both Labour and Conservative pledged to build one million homes.
[3 marks – accurate point with development and exemplification]

People choose not to vote because they don't identify with one of the main political parties. They view the party policies as being very similar eg in 2017 both Labour and Conservative pledged to build one million homes. This may have contributed to around one in three people choosing not to vote.
[4 marks – accurate point with development, exemplification and analysis]

Credit reference to aspects of the following:

- basic right not to vote
- voter apathy
- have not registered
- safe seats
- lack of trust in MPs/political system
- lack of role models
- alternative outlets for participation eg pressure groups.

(b) *Candidates can be credited in a number of ways up to a maximum of 8 marks.*

Possible approaches to answering the question:

The Prime Minister is very powerful because they are the leader of the largest party in the House of Commons.

[1 mark – accurate but undeveloped point]

The Prime Minister is very powerful because they are the leader of the largest party in the House of Commons.

In 2017, Theresa May was returned as Prime Minister with 318 MPs.

[2 marks – accurate point with development]

The Prime Minister is very powerful because they are the leader of the largest party in the House of Commons.

In 2017, Theresa May was returned as Prime Minister with 318 MPs. This was more than any other party and allows the Prime Minister to implement government legislation eg Brexit.

[4 marks – accurate point with development, exemplification and analysis]

Credit reference to aspects of the following:

- power of appointment – hiring and firing ministers
- honours list
- Executive head
- chairing the Cabinet and setting the Cabinet agenda
- media attention
- relationships with foreign leaders.

7. *Candidates can be credited in a number of ways up to a maximum of 10 marks.*

Possible approaches to answering the question:

Support

I can support the view of Archie Murray when he states 'there is widespread support for replacing the current system used to elect MPs... in the House of Commons' because Source 3 shows that Green MP Caroline Lucas states 'the movement for a fairer voting system is stronger than ever'.

[1 mark – accurate use of Source 3 but minimal development]

I can support the view of Archie Murray when he states 'there is widespread support for replacing the current system used to elect MPs... in the House of Commons' because Source 3 shows that Green MP Caroline Lucas states 'the movement for a fairer voting system is stronger than ever.' This can be linked within Source 1 because it explains that Lucas' Private Members' Bill for electoral reform received cross-party support from five different political parties.

[2 marks – accurate use of Source 1 and Source 3 linking two pieces of evidence]

I can support the view of Archie Murray when he states 'there is widespread support for replacing the current system used to elect MPs... in the House of Commons' because Source 1 shows that there has been a rise in popularity of reform groups supporting changing the way we elect MPs. This can be linked to Source 3 where

Iain Thorpe from Earth News states they will continue to campaign against the use of first-past-the-post in UK elections and work with a cross-party group of MPs calling for immediate action. This shows that people are still unhappy and will continue to campaign for change.

[3 marks – accurate information linked from two sources with some evaluation of the information ie 'this shows...'].

Credit reference to aspects of the following:

- increasing support for changing the voting system. 25% in 2005 but by 2017 this had increased to just over 40% [nearly doubled] [Source 2]
- views of Molly Miller 'growing tide of support for change' [Source 3]
- Electoral Reform Society has supported the idea of changing the system used for voting since 1884 [Source 3]
- Private Members' Bill supported by five different political parties linked to Source 3 detailing support from Labour UKIP, SNP, Liberal Democrats and Greens [Source 1]
- Labour MP voicing support for the Electoral Reform Bill [Source 3].

Oppose

Possible approaches to answering the question.

I can oppose the view of Archie Murray when he states 'there is widespread support for replacing the current system used to elect MPs in the House of Commons' because Source 1 states opponents to change argue that the 'public want to retain the current system as they recognised that it works'.

[1 mark – accurate use of Source 1 but minimal development]

I can oppose the view of Archie Murray when he states 'there is widespread support for replacing the current system used to elect MPs in the House of Commons' because Source 1 states opponents to change argue that the 'public want to retain the current system as they recognise that it works'. This can be linked to Source 2 that shows that in 2017 over half of those surveyed did not want electoral reform for General Elections.

[2 marks – accurate use of sources 1 & 2 that links two pieces of evidence]

I can oppose the view of Archie Murray when he states 'there is widespread support for replacing the current system used to elect MPs in the House of Commons' because Source 3 states that the Private Members' Bill put forward by Caroline Lucas was voted down in the House of Commons by 81 to 74 votes, demonstrating that there is not widespread support for replacing the current system. This can be linked to Source 2 which further proves this point as it shows that in the referendum on replacing the current system the majority of voters said 'no'. In total, a substantial 13 million voters, more than double that of the yes voters, did not support for replacing the current system.

[3 marks – accurate information linked from two sources with some evaluative language ie 'majority' 'substantial' 'more than double']

Credit reference to aspects of the following:

- supporters argue FPTP has many benefits, eg simple to use and stable governments [Source 1]
- desire for change not supported by current government and opposition [Source 1]
- 13,013,123 voters said 'No' to changing the parliamentary voting system [Source 2]

- Joe Charlton 'we have already had a referendum that delivered a decisive decision' & 'the government is right not to support any change' [Source 3]
- Niamh Armour 'if we move to PR then extremist parties will gain power...' [Source 3].

Part C: Social Inequality

8. *Candidates can be credited in a number of ways **up to a maximum of 4 marks.***

Possible approaches to answering the question:

Private Sector

Private companies can build housing for low income groups.

> [1 mark – accurate but undeveloped point]

Private companies can build housing for low income groups. Housing developers are often required to build a specified number of affordable homes in new developments.

> [2 marks – accurate point with development]

Private companies can build housing for low income groups. Housing developers build a specified number of affordable homes and then work with the local council and the Scottish government [through the Scottish Futures Trust] who buy the homes and lets them to tenants at affordable rent.

> [3 marks – accurate point with development and exemplification]

Credit reference to aspects of the following:
- positive discrimination policies to encourage minority groups
- Asda's diversity and inclusion policy ensures there is no discrimination in terms of age, gender, ethnicity, sexual orientation or disability
- B&Q actively recruits from all age groups and, with 28% of its workforce over the age of 50, it has many employees who are semi-retired
- Sainsbury's actively tries to recruit more 'mature' workers across Britain
- providing good benefits eg maternity pay, family and sick pay
- TSB employees receive 4% on top of their basic salary to spend on tax-efficient benefits such as childcare or critical illness cover. Workers are each allowed two paid days a year for voluntary work and the firm allows flexible working hours. Parents are encouraged to attend their children's nativity plays and sports days
- Iceland frozen food chain made sure frontline staff were paid at least 2% above the national living wage and abolished its lower rate for new starters
- working with the government in joint projects which create jobs in railways, construction [eg building and maintaining roads and highways]. In Scotland, this is now called Non-profit distributing [NPD] and replaces PPI.

Voluntary Sector

Voluntary sector has charity shops which raise funds to help deprived groups.

> [1 mark – accurate but undeveloped point]

Voluntary sector charities, such as Oxfam and Save the Children, have shops which raise funds to help deprived groups.

> [2 marks – accurate point with development]

Voluntary sector charities, such as Oxfam and Save the Children, have shops which raise funds to help deprived groups.

They also give opportunities to volunteers to build skills and confidence which will help them get a job.

> [3 marks – accurate point with development and exemplification]

Credit reference to aspects of the following:
- research and publish reports, recommendations to the government about tackling poverty and disadvantage eg Joseph Rowntree Foundation
- some charities, eg Trussell Trust, provide food through a network of food banks across the UK. They can provide 3 days emergency food to families who are struggling to afford basic food items
- provide advice eg Age Concern provides information and advice over their helpline eg helping people find out the benefits they are entitled to claim
- befriending services eg Scope run befriending services for families of disabled people and they provide emotional and practical support to struggling parents
- Comic Relief raises millions of pounds, mainly through two big fundraising campaigns: Red Nose Day and Sport Relief and give these to charity and voluntary organisations around the UK.

9. *Candidates can be credited in a number of ways **up to a maximum of 6 marks.***

Possible approaches to answering the question:

Social and economic inequality continues to exist because some people have a better paying job.

> [1 mark – accurate but undeveloped point]

Social and economic inequality continues to exist because some people have a better paying job eg a doctor is paid more than a hospital porter.

> [2 marks – accurate point with development]

Social and economic inequality continues to exist because some people have a better paying job eg a doctor is paid more than a hospital porter. This means that the doctor can choose to live in more affluent areas.

> [3 marks – accurate point with development and analysis]

Credit reference to aspects of the following:
- unemployment
- skills and experience
- number of dependent children
- education/training
- poor health: unable to work due to illness
- racial discrimination
- gender discrimination
- criminal record makes it difficult to find work
- access to healthcare
- housing/environment
- inheritance.

10. *Candidates can be credited in a number of ways **up to a maximum of 6 marks.***

Possible approaches to answering the question:

Social and economic inequality has a negative consequence on families because they may feel socially excluded.

> [1 mark – accurate but undeveloped point]

Social and economic inequality has a negative consequence on families because they may feel socially excluded. For example, they may not be able to afford certain school trips for their children.

> [2 marks – accurate point with development]

Social and economic inequality has a negative consequence on families because they may feel socially excluded. For example, they may not be able to afford certain school trips for their children. This could lead to the children feeling isolated, developing low self-esteem and being victims of bullying. This applies to almost one in four children in the UK.

[4 marks – accurate point with development, exemplification and analysis]

Credit reference to aspects of the following:
- cycle of poverty
- poor health [physical and mental]
- poor housing
- underperformance in education
- the cost to wider society eg taxation
- crime.

Part D: Crime and the Law

11. *Candidates can be credited in a number of ways **up to a maximum of 4 marks**.*

Possible approaches to answering the question:

One way that perpetrators can be affected by crime is that they can be given a prison sentence.

[1 mark – accurate but undeveloped point]

One way that perpetrators can be affected by crime is that they can be given a prison sentence. If given a prison sentence, perpetrators may then lose contact with their family and friends.

[2 marks – accurate point with development]

One way that perpetrators can be affected by crime is that they can be given a prison sentence. If given a prison sentence, perpetrators may then lose contact with their family and friends. This could then lead to isolation and mental health issues which may hinder their rehabilitation.

[3 marks – accurate point with development and analysis]

Credit reference to aspects of the following:
- mental health issues
- loss of family and support network
- unemployment
- financial issues – fines/mortgage payments will fall behind
- homelessness
- media publicity/public humiliation/embarrassment
- lack of career opportunities
- removal from university/college courses
- decreasing opportunities for friendships and dating relationships
- trapped in the cycle of crime.

12. *Candidates can be credited in a number of ways **up to a maximum of 6 marks**.*

Possible approaches to answering the question:

One reason why some people commit crime as a result of economic issues is due to the fact that they cannot afford to meet their basic needs.

[1 mark – accurate but undeveloped point]

One reason why some people commit crime as a result of economic issues is due to the fact that they cannot afford to meet their basic needs. This may be due to the fact that they are unemployed.

[2 marks – accurate point with development]

One reason why some people commit crime as a result of economic issues is due to the fact that they cannot afford to meet their basic needs. This may be due to the fact that they are unemployed. People who are unemployed

may then suffer from food poverty and could turn to shoplifting in order to survive. For example, benefit sanctions may cause a single mother to turn to shoplifting to provide for her children.

[4 marks – accurate point with development, exemplification and analysis]

Credit reference to aspects of the following:
- poverty
- broken windows theory
- greed
- strain theory
- social exclusion.

13. *Candidates can be credited in a number of ways **up to a maximum of 6 marks**.*

Possible approaches to answering the question:

Prisons are effective as they remove dangerous people from society.

[1 mark – accurate but undeveloped point]

Prisons are effective as they remove dangerous people from society. People who commit murders are given life sentences.

[2 marks – accurate point with development]

Prisons are effective as they remove dangerous people from society. People who commit murders are given life sentences and are often sent to high security prisons, such as HMP Shotts. This means that people in society feel reassured and the perpetrator is given opportunity for rehabilitation.

[4 marks – accurate point with development, exemplification and analysis]

Credit reference to aspects of the following:
- deterrence
- rehabilitation
- retribution
- punishment.

14. *Candidates can be credited in a number of ways **up to a maximum of 10 marks**.*

Possible approaches to answering the question:

Option 1: The Scottish Government should build a prison for elderly prisoners.

The Scottish Government should build a new prison for elderly prisoners. Evidence to support this can be found in Source 2 where it states that 'Purpose built prisons for the elderly are the only solution: prisoners' human rights are not being met!' This is further backed up in Source 3 where it states 'Frail and ill, older prisoners are being denied their human rights. They often struggle to carry out the most basic daily tasks, such as carrying their meals back to their cells and washing themselves.'

[2 marks – evidence linked from Source 2 and Source 3]

Credit reference to aspects of the following:
- recently there has been increasing evidence that the physical needs of elderly prisoners are not being met in current prisons, as the buildings are not suitable [Source 1]
- most prisons are designed for the young and able. In the UK, there is only one prison that has a wing specifically designed for the elderly [Source 1]
- most prison buildings are multi-storey with only stairs and no lifts. Many have narrow doors and corridors. The conditions the prisoners have to live in make for a particularly intimidating and inaccessible environment for elderly prisoners [Source 1]

- in March 2017, there were 102 prisoners aged over 80 in Scotland, and 5 who were 90 or older. These types of prisoners have needs that are constantly changing and a purpose built prison would help to meet their needs [Source 1]
- 'Surge in pension-age prisoners: Specially designed cells as part of a new state of the art pensioner prison are desperately needed to cope with elderly crime wave' [Source 2]
- elderly prisoner numbers have increased from 660 in 2011 to approximately 750 in 2017 [Source 2]
- 'A purpose built prison is the only solution, no matter what the cost' [Source 2]
- a purpose built prison is the only solution to the constantly increasing number of elderly prisoners and this is likely to be more of a challenge in the future as prison numbers are increasing and our prisons are already overcrowded [Source 3].

Reasons for rejecting other option:

I did not choose Option 2 as although some people may say that 'Even basic building changes such as installing a stairlift, would solve many of the issues that elderly prisoners have.' [Source 3], this is not true as in Source 3 it also says 'Adapting current prisons is not an option as the buildings are not wheelchair friendly and so many structural changes would need to take place, this would be very costly'.

[2 marks awarded for using two pieces of information from Source 3 to form a rebuttal. Do not credit if marks have already been awarded for this point]

Option 2: The Scottish Government should adapt existing prisons for elderly prisoners.

The Scottish Government should adapt existing prisons to meet the needs of elderly prisoners as in Source 2 it states that 'Adapting prisons to meet elderly prisoners' needs would cost much less than building a new purpose built prison for the elderly'.

[1 mark – evidence drawn from Source 2]

The Scottish Government should adapt current prisons to meet the needs of elderly prisoners as in Source 2 it states 'Adapting prisons to meet elderly prisoners' needs would cost much less than building a new purpose built prison for the elderly' and Source 3 states 'The Government does not have the funding to build new purpose built prisons for the elderly'.

[2 marks – evidence linked from Sources 2 and 3]

Credit reference to aspects of the following:
- the Scottish Prison Service [SPS] has 13 publicly managed prisons and 2 privately run prisons. There have been some changes made to these buildings to cater for elderly prisoners and this has made life easier for some [Source 1]
- one prison has tried to accommodate these prisoners; they have put in a stairlift and adapted 10 of their cells to meet elderly people's needs. This cost the Government £560,000 but has made a massive difference to elderly prisoners' lives [Source 1]
- '94 year old prisoner dies in his cell after falling out of his bed. Bed guards could have saved his life' [Source 2]
- 'Adapting prisons to meet elderly prisoners' needs would cost much less than building a new purpose built prison for the elderly' [Source 2]
- adapting prisons is a much more economical solution to the problem [Source 3]

- even basic building changes such as installing a stairlift, would solve many of the issues that elderly prisoners have. The average cost of installing a stairlift is £3,475 [Source 3].

Reasons for rejecting the other option:

Although some people would argue that building a purpose built prison for elderly prisoners is the best option, this would cost £250 million [Source 3]. Therefore, Option 1 is not the correct choice as Source 2 states that 'Adapting prisons to meet elderly prisoners' needs would cost much less than building a new purpose built prison for the elderly'. This is further backed up in Source 3 where it states that even really basic building changes like putting a stairlift in, would solve many of the issues that elderly prisoners have. The average cost of putting a stairlift in is £3,475. This shows that there are much more economical solutions to the issues arising from an elderly prison population as even fitting a stairlift in each of the prisons in Scotland would cost less than building a purpose built prison.

[3 marks – evidence drawn from two sources, with evaluative comment]

Part E: World Powers

15. *Candidates can be credited in a number of ways **up to a maximum of 4 marks**.*

Possible approaches to answering the question:

Many countries rely on China for trade.

[1 mark – accurate but undeveloped point]

Many countries rely on China for trade. Australia relies on China to buy minerals from them.

[2 marks – accurate point with development]

Many countries rely on China for trade. Australia relies on China to buy minerals from them. 13% of Australia's exports are thermal coal to China.

[3 marks – accurate point with development and exemplification]

Credit reference to aspects of the following:
- trade
- imports/exports
- finance/banking
- financial aid
- services.

16. *Candidates can be credited in a number of ways **up to a maximum of 6 marks**.*

Possible approaches to answering the question:

The Canadian Government has tried to reduce social inequalities by encouraging people to make better lifestyle choices.

[1 mark – accurate but undeveloped point]

The USA has tried to reduce social inequalities in health by providing help with buying food. SNAP cost the US government $70.9 billion per year.

[2 marks – accurate point with development]

The Chinese Government have launched Healthy China 2020. This is a plan to provide universal healthcare coverage for all Chinese people. The Chinese Government have allocated billions more in spending to support this plan.

[3 marks – accurate point with development and exemplification]

Credit reference to aspects of the following:
- health: passing laws, providing free health care, issuing public guidelines [smoking/exercise/healthy eating]
- education: benefits to encourage students to stay at school; student loans; scholarships and bursaries; investment in education
- housing: social housing; help with housing costs
- anti-discrimination legislation
- welfare benefits
- crime reduction
- employment schemes.

17. *Candidates can be credited in a number of ways up to a maximum of 6 marks.*

Possible approaches to answering the question:

China

Some people are poorly represented in government as they are not in the Communist Party.
[1 mark – accurate but undeveloped point]

Those living and working in rural areas are poorly represented in national government as they are less likely to be members of the Communist Party. The rural Chinese can take part in local committees but these tend to only focus on local issues and not on provincial, national or international issues.
[3 marks – accurate point with development and exemplification]

Credit reference to aspects of the following:
- income/poverty
- urban/rural divide
- gender – national government still dominated by men
- party membership is limited and has restrictions
- migrant workers may not be registered and cannot participate
- those with anti-communist views or those who support democratic reform are not well represented and are often silenced by the authorities
- pressure group activists are not represented especially if they oppose the Communist system.

USA

Black Americans are not well represented as there are few Black role models in government.
[1 mark – accurate but undeveloped point]

Black Americans are not well represented as they are more likely to be poor. This tends to mean that they are less likely to run for office.
[2 marks – accurate point with development]

Hispanic Americans are less likely to be represented in government as there is a much lower participation rate among Hispanics. Some have difficulty as English is not their first language so politics and government is difficult for them to understand. This leads to fewer Latinos being elected to a high office position such as Governor or Senator.
[3 marks – accurate point with development and exemplification]

Credit reference to aspects of the following:
- low paid unskilled work/white collar jobs. Difference in participation leads to difference in representation
- Blacks and Hispanics experience social and economic inequality as a result of poverty. Apathetic, few role models, other priorities. Greater representation in local elections

- women remain underrepresented as they either do not run for office or are not chosen by the big two parties, despite the fact that women are more likely to vote in presidential elections
- poorly educated are poorly represented and are less likely to vote
- some recent immigrants may not have legal status and may lack representation as a result
- homeless people may be unlikely to vote and lack representation.

Part F: World Issues

18. *Candidates can be credited in a number of ways up to a maximum of 4 marks.*

Possible approaches to answering the question:

Nationalism is one of the main causes of terrorism.
[1 mark – accurate but undeveloped point]

Nationalism is one of the main causes of terrorism as some people want independence for the area they live in but feel they cannot get this peacefully.
[2 marks – accurate point with development]

Nationalism is one of the main causes of terrorism as some people want independence for the area they live in but feel they cannot get this peacefully. For example, ETA have fought for the independence of the Basque region of Spain.
[3 marks – accurate point with development and exemplification]

Credit reference to aspects of the following:
- religion
- revenge
- corrupt Governments
- Civil War
- poor health – HIV
- poor education
- debt
- trade
- nuclear proliferation.

19. *Candidates can be credited in a number of ways up to a maximum of 6 marks.*

Possible approaches to answering the question:

Issue - Underdevelopment in Africa

The UN sends emergency relief aid.
[1 mark – accurate but undeveloped point]

The UN sends emergency relief aid to assist with disasters such as famine and drought, and has sent items such as medical supplies and food.
[2 marks – accurate point with development]

UNICEF works as part of the UN to improve the lives of children. It is working with schools to help improve rates of literacy and has a campaign called Schools for Africa to help some of the millions of children in Africa who do not get the chance to go to school because of war, poverty or discrimination.
[3 marks – accurate with development and exemplification]

Credit reference to aspects of the following:
- food/water/emergency relief
- medical equipment/experts/medicines/vaccinations
- peace talks/treaty negotiations
- economic sanctions
- UN resolutions
- economic aid

- specialist workers – engineers, scientists etc
- financial aid through the World Bank
- UN may hold peace talks eg with Syrian government during times of conflict. Pressure for government to resign
- military action by NATO
- peacekeeping operations.

20. *Candidates can be credited in a number of ways **up to a maximum of 6 marks.***

Possible approaches to answering the question:

Civil war has an impact on other countries because they will have to deal with refugees.
[1 mark – accurate but undeveloped point]

Civil war has an impact on other countries because they will have to deal with refugees. Many civilians try to escape the war and cross the border into other countries which have to provide shelter.
[2 marks – accurate point with development]

Civil war has an impact on other countries because they will have to deal with refugees. Many civilians try to escape the war and cross the border into other countries which have to provide shelter. For example, many have fled Syria to escape the war to countries such as Greece.
[3 marks – accurate with development and exemplification]

Credit reference to aspects of the following:
- membership of NATO means country can be expected to go to war
- creates instability within your country
- membership of UN means countries have to pay to provide aid
- economic refugees
- effects of mass migration
- pressure placed on government to provide aid for humanitarian reasons
- effect of terrorism.

21. *Candidates can be credited in a number of ways **up to a maximum of 10 marks.***

Possible approaches to answering the question:

The importance of the military to the Indonesian Government

Conclusion: The military are not seen as important to the Indonesian Government.
[1 mark – valid conclusion]

Conclusion: The military are not seen as important to the Indonesian Government.

Evidence: This is supported by Source 1 which shows Indonesia is ranked 116th in the world for military spending.
[2 marks – conclusion and evidence from one source]

Conclusion: The military are not seen as important to the Indonesian Government.

Evidence: This is supported by Source 1 which shows Indonesia is ranked 116th in the world for military spending and further by Source 2 where South Sudan spends far more of its GDP on the military [10·3% of its GDP] compared to only 0·9% of Indonesia's GDP.
[3 marks – conclusion and information from two sources with evaluative terminology]

The importance of Indonesia's exports

Conclusion: Indonesia has some very important exports.
[1 mark – valid conclusion]

Conclusion: Indonesia has some very important exports.

Evidence: Source 3 states that Indonesia is the world's biggest producer of palm oil, farming over 6 million hectares.
[2 marks – conclusion and evidence from one source]

Conclusion: Indonesia has some very important exports.

Evidence: Source 3 states that Indonesia is the world's biggest producer of palm oil, farming over 6 million hectares, it exports 14·4 billion dollars worth of palm oil compared to Malaysia which only exports 9·1 billion dollars worth. This is over 5 billion dollars more.
[3 marks – conclusion and two pieces of evidence from one source and evaluation]

Indonesia's influence within alliances

Conclusion: Indonesia is very influential within alliances.
[1 mark – valid conclusion]

Conclusion: Indonesia is very influential within alliances.

Evidence: Source 1 shows that Indonesia is a member of several important alliances such as the G20 and the UN.
[2 marks – conclusion and evidence from one source]

Conclusion: Indonesia is very influential within alliances.

Evidence: Source 1 shows that Indonesia is a member of several important alliances such as the G20 and the UN. Indonesia is the only ASEAN member of the G20 according to Source 3, which gives it more influence than other Asian countries.
[3 marks – conclusion and information from two sources]

The importance of tourism to Indonesia
- Conclusion: Tourism is very important to Indonesia.
[1 mark – valid conclusion]
- Conclusion: Tourism is very important to Indonesia.
- Evidence: Source 2 shows that tourism brings in almost 10 billion dollars to the economy.
[2 marks – conclusion and evidence from one source]

Conclusion: Tourism is very important to Indonesia.

Evidence: Source 2 shows that tourism brings in almost 10 billion dollars to the economy. This links to Source 3 which states the government has also set up a department to promote tourism which is significant as it must view it as important.
[3 marks – conclusion and information from two sources with evaluation]

NATIONAL 5 MODERN STUDIES 2019

Part A: Democracy in Scotland

1. *Candidates can be credited in a number of ways **up to a maximum of 4 marks.***

Possible approaches to answering the question:

The Scottish Parliament is responsible for the matter of education.
[1 mark — accurate but undeveloped point]

The Scottish Parliament is responsible for the matter of education. MSPs can discuss and make changes to the education system in Scotland.
[2 marks — accurate point with development]

The Scottish Parliament is responsible for the matter of education. MSPs can discuss and make changes to the education system in Scotland. For example, the Scottish Parliament Education and Skills committee is currently investigating how successful Curriculum for Excellence has been.

[3 marks — accurate point with development and exemplification]

Credit reference to aspects of the following:
- devolved matters such as agriculture, forestry and fisheries
- environment
- health and social services
- housing
- law and order
- local government
- sport and the arts
- tourism and economic development
- aspects of transport.

2. *Candidates can be credited in a number of ways **up to a maximum of 6 marks.***

Possible approaches to answering the question:

Individuals in Scotland have the right to protest.
[1 mark — accurate but undeveloped point]

Individuals in Scotland have the right to protest. They can hold demonstrations against laws they disagree with.
[2 marks — accurate point with development]

Individuals in Scotland have the right to protest. They can hold demonstrations against laws they disagree with. For example, people who disagreed with the Offensive Behaviour at Football Act, such as the pressure group Fans Against Criminalisation, held marches and demonstrations in Glasgow as part of their protests against this law.
[3 marks — accurate point with development and exemplification]

Credit reference to aspects of the following:
- the right to a fair trial
- the right to privacy
- the right to vote
- the right to education and healthcare
- the right to join a pressure group
- the right to join a political party
- the right to protest
- the right to lobby a representative
- freedom of expression
- freedom of religion or conscience
- freedom of assembly
- freedom from torture, inhuman or degrading treatment and slavery.

3. *Candidates can be credited in a number of ways **up to a maximum of 6 marks.***

Possible approaches to answering the question:

Political parties use the media during election campaigns in Scotland to gain support.
[1 mark — accurate but undeveloped point]

Political parties use the media during election campaigns in Scotland to gain support. They hope this will give them a better chance of winning the election.
[2 marks — accurate point with development]

Political parties use the media during election campaigns in Scotland to gain support. They hope this will give them a better chance of winning the election. For example, during an election campaign, Scottish Labour may use social media such as YouTube to promote their policies by posting short video clips.
[3 marks — accurate point with development and exemplification]

Political parties use the media during election campaigns in Scotland to gain support. They hope this will give them a better chance of winning the election. For example, during an election campaign, Scottish Labour may use social media such as YouTube to promote their policies by posting short video clips. This method appeared to be successful for the Labour Party during the 2017 general election as many younger voters who voted Labour said they were influenced by social media.
[4 marks — accurate point with development, exemplification and analysis]

Part B: Democracy in the United Kingdom

4. *Candidates can be credited in a number of ways **up to a maximum of 4 marks.***

Possible approaches to answering the question:

The UK Parliament is responsible for the matter of defence.
[1 mark — accurate but undeveloped point]

The UK Parliament is responsible for the matter of defence. This means that the UK Parliament makes decisions about how best to protect the UK against terrorist attacks.
[2 marks — accurate point with development]

The UK Parliament is responsible for the matter of defence. This means that the UK Parliament makes decisions about how best to protect the UK against terrorist attacks. For example, the UK Parliament passed the 2015 Counter Terrorism and Security Act which prevents individuals travelling abroad to engage in terrorist activities.
[3 marks — accurate point with development and exemplification]

Credit reference to aspects of the following:
- the constitution
- benefits and Social Security
- employment
- immigration
- foreign policy
- equal opportunities
- broadcasting.

5. *Candidates can be credited in a number of ways **up to a maximum of 6 marks.***

Possible approaches to answering the question:

Individuals have the right to vote in a democracy.
[1 mark — accurate but undeveloped point]

Individuals have the right to vote in a democracy. Individuals can vote in elections or referendums.
[2 marks — accurate point with development]

Individuals have the right to vote in a democracy. Individuals can vote in elections or referendums. For example, 32 million individuals voted in the 2017 general election.
[3 marks — accurate point with development and exemplification]

Credit reference to aspects of the following:

- the right to a fair trial
- the right to privacy
- the right to vote
- the right to education and healthcare
- the right to join a pressure group
- the right to join a political party
- the right to protest
- the right to lobby a representative
- freedom of expression
- freedom of religion or conscience
- freedom of assembly
- freedom from torture, inhuman or degrading treatment and slavery.

6. *Candidates can be credited in a number of ways **up to a maximum of 6 marks.***

Possible approaches to answering the question:

Political parties use the media during election campaigns because it allows the party to spread their election message.

[1 mark — accurate but undeveloped point]

Political parties use the media during election campaigns because it allows the party to spread their election message. Using traditional media and social media allows political parties to reach millions of voters to tell them about their manifesto promises.

[2 marks — accurate point with development]

Political parties use the media during election campaigns because it allows the party to spread their election message. Using traditional media and social media allows political parties to reach millions of voters to tell them about their manifesto promises. For example, the BBC leaders' TV debate during the 2017 general election campaign was watched by an average of 3·5 million viewers.

[3 marks — accurate point with development and exemplification]

Political parties use the media during election campaigns because it allows the party to spread their election message. Using traditional media and social media allows political parties to reach millions of voters to tell them about their manifesto promises. For example, the BBC leaders' TV debate during the 2017 general election campaign was watched by an average of 3·5 million viewers.

The five leaders who took part debated issues such as health, education and Brexit with the aim of persuading voters to cast their vote in favour of their party.

[4 marks — accurate point with development, exemplification and analysis]

Credit reference to aspects of the following:

- engage with younger voters via social media platforms
- use of 'attack' advertising to discredit opposition
- create publicity for the campaign message via soundbites
- Party Election Broadcasts (PEBs) promote manifesto pledges to voters
- printed press allegiance supports campaign at expense of other parties
- mobilise grassroot supporters via social media to organise local campaigns
- deliver campaign messages to those unable to be reached through traditional methods, such as canvassing, to attempt to increase turnout.

7. *Candidates can be credited in a number of ways **up to a maximum of 10 marks.***

Possible approaches to answering the question:

The trends in UK trade union membership

Conclusion: Trade union membership in the UK has decreased.

[1 mark — valid conclusion]

Conclusion: Trade union membership in the UK has decreased.

Evidence: In Source 2 it shows that in 2008, trade union membership was just over 7 million but by 2018 it had fallen to just over 6 million.

[2 marks — conclusion and evidence from one source]

Conclusion: Trade union membership in the UK has decreased.

Evidence: In Source 2 it shows that in 2008 trade union membership was just over 7 million but by 2018 it had fallen to just over 6 million. This can be linked to Source 1 that states that trade union membership was once as high as 13·2 million, meaning that membership has more than halved in total since the late 1970s.

[3 marks — conclusion and evidence from two sources with evaluative terminology]

The rate of UK trade union membership compared to European countries

Conclusion: Trade union membership in the UK is higher than many other European countries.

[1 mark — valid conclusion]

Conclusion: Trade union membership in the UK is higher than many other European countries.

Evidence: In Source 1 it shows that just under 25% of all workers in the UK are members of trade unions. According to Source 3, this is higher than many other European countries such as Germany, Poland, France and Lithuania.

[2 marks — conclusion and evidence from two sources]

Conclusion: Trade union membership in the UK is higher than many other European countries.

Evidence: In Source 1 it shows that just under 25% of all workers in the UK are members of trade unions. According to Source 3, this is higher than many other European countries such as Germany, France and Lithuania. France has only 8% of employees in trade unions, this is around 17% lower than the UK which is a significant difference.

[3 marks — conclusion and evidence from two sources with evaluative terminology]

Gender composition of trade union membership in the UK

Conclusion: Women are more likely than men to belong to a trade union in the UK.

[1 mark — valid conclusion]

Conclusion: Women are more likely than men to belong to a trade union in the UK.

Evidence: In Source 1 it states that women are more likely to belong to a trade union then men and in some trade unions, such as Unison, women account for the majority of members.

[2 marks — conclusion and evidence from one source]

Conclusion: Women are more likely than men to belong to a trade union in the UK.

Evidence: In Source 1 it states that women are more likely to belong to a trade union than men and in some trade unions, such as Unison, women account for the majority of members. This can be supported by Source 2 that shows female membership in the last ten years is consistently higher than male membership. For example, in 2018, 25% of women belonged to a trade union which was 5% higher than the rate for male membership.

[3 marks — conclusion and information from two sources with evaluative terminology]

The difference in trade union membership between Scotland and England

Conclusion: Trade union membership is higher in Scotland than in England.

[1 mark — valid conclusion]

Conclusion: Trade union membership is higher in Scotland than in England.

Evidence: Source 1 states trade union membership in Scotland is close to 30% but Source 3 shows England's trade union membership rate is less than 25%.

[2 marks — conclusion and evidence from two sources]

Conclusion: Trade union membership is higher in Scotland than in England.

Evidence: Source 1 states trade union membership in Scotland is close to 30% but Source 3 shows England's trade union membership rate is less than 25%. This shows that employees in England are less likely to belong to a trade union than employees in Scotland.

[3 marks — conclusion and information from two sources with evaluative terminology]

Part C: Social Inequality

8. *Candidates can be credited in a number of ways **up to a maximum of 4 marks**.*

Possible approaches to answering the question:

When there is a lot of poverty in a community then it might lead to people leaving the area.

[1 mark — accurate but undeveloped point]

When there is a lot of poverty in a community then it might lead to people leaving the area. People will have to move to find work and this means that there will be less people paying their council tax.

[2 marks — accurate point with development]

When there is a lot of poverty in a community then it might lead to people leaving the area. People will have to move to find work and this means that there will be less people paying their council tax. This then means that it will be difficult for councils to provide services like libraries, swimming pools and schools.

[3 marks — accurate point with development and exemplification]

Credit reference to aspects of the following:
- businesses leave
- lower educational attainment
- higher crime rates, for example vandalism and anti-social behaviour
- unemployment
- house prices go down
- rates of social exclusion increase which has an impact on health services.

9. *Candidates can be credited in a number of ways **up to a maximum of 6 marks**.*

Possible approaches to answering the question:

One way that highlights that inequality is a problem in the UK is child poverty.

[1 mark — accurate but undeveloped point]

One way that highlights that inequality is a problem in the UK is child poverty. In March 2018 it was estimated that over 4 million children in the UK lived in poverty.

[2 marks — accurate point with development]

One way that highlights that inequality is a problem in the UK is child poverty. In March 2018 it was estimated that over 4 million children in the UK lived in poverty. The Child Poverty Action Group suggests that this is due to benefit cuts and reduction in tax credits.

[3 marks — accurate point with development and exemplification]

Credit reference to aspects of the following:
- unemployment
- homelessness
- gender pay gap
- health inequalities.

10. (a) *Candidates can be credited in a number of ways **up to a maximum of 8 marks**.*

Possible approaches to answering the question:

Private companies have tackled social and economic inequality by working in partnership with the Scottish Government to provide jobs.

[1 mark — accurate but undeveloped point]

Private companies have tackled social and economic inequality by working in partnership with the Scottish Government to provide jobs and apprenticeships. Modern Apprenticeships are for people aged over 16 and helps them into paid employment.

[2 marks — accurate point with development]

Private companies have tackled social and economic inequality by working in partnership with the Scottish Government to provide apprenticeships. Modern Apprenticeships are for people aged over 16 which helps them into paid employment and gives them training which could lead to further qualifications such as an SVQ in Business Administration or Joinery.

This is seen as a very successful way of reducing the number of NEETs (Not in Employment Education or Training) and these are valued by employers when the apprentice is looking to further their career.

[4 marks — accurate point with development, exemplification and analysis]

Credit reference to aspects of the following:
- more women on boards of private companies
- affordable housing
- private sector initiatives, for example Sainsbury's have a 'slow shopping' day
- flexible working hours
- non-discriminatory policies
- financial incentives, for example childcare subsidy.

(b) *Candidates can be credited in a number of ways **up to a maximum of 8 marks**.*

Possible approaches to answering the question:

Discrimination affects women because it means they are less likely to get promotion.

[1 mark — accurate but undeveloped point]

Discrimination affects women because it means they are less likely to get promotion compared to men. This means that they are less likely to have high paying jobs.

[2 marks — accurate point with development]

Discrimination affects women because it means they are less likely to get promotion compared to men. This means that they are less likely to have high paying jobs. This might be because employers are worried they may take time off to have children. Evidence has shown that mothers who return to work end up earning a third less than men and face a 'glass ceiling' when going for promotion. Although there are now more women on boards of FTSE 100 companies than in the past showing that there has been improvement.

[4 marks — accurate point with development, exemplification and analysis]

Credit reference to aspects of the following:

Women
- more likely to take time out of career for children/be unemployed
- more likely to live in poverty
- can face harassment in the workplace, for example evidence of sexual harassment in parliament/film industry recently
- less likely to stand as candidates in elections, poorer levels of political representation.

Minority ethnic groups
- a 'glass door' which leads to higher levels of unemployment
- racist attitudes
- harassment and intimidation
- lower wage levels
- under represented in many jobs and in politics
- lack of role models
- more likely to have poorer housing.

Elderly
- can face abuse/harassment/victimisation
- unequal treatment in healthcare, for example rationing of care
- ageism.

Social class
- more likely to turn to crime
- stigma
- more likely to have poor mental health.

Part D: Crime and the Law

11. *Candidates can be credited in a number of ways **up to a maximum of 4 marks.***

Possible approaches to answering the question:

Some people believe that criminals are 'born evil'.
[1 mark — accurate but undeveloped point]

Some people believe that criminals are 'born evil' and that they are physiologically distinct from noncriminals.
[2 marks — accurate point with development]

Some people believe that criminals are 'born evil' and that they are physiologically distinct from noncriminals. For example, they would argue that criminals have no choice, it is 'nature' and they have no control over it.
[3 marks — accurate point with development and exemplification]

Credit reference to aspects of the following:
- nature versus nurture
- bio-chemical conditions such as hormone imbalance
- warrior gene (MAOA)
- neuro-physical conditions such as learning difficulties
- intelligence
- sex
- mental health issues.

12. *Candidates can be credited in a number of ways **up to a maximum of 6 marks.***

Possible approaches to answering the question:

One way that highlights that crime is a problem in the UK is the increase in knife crime.
[1 mark — accurate but undeveloped point]

One way that highlights that crime is a problem in the UK is the increase in knife crime. In September 2018 knife crime had risen to the highest level in England and Wales since 2010.
[2 marks — accurate point with development]

One way that highlights that crime is a problem in the UK is the increase in knife crime. In September 2018 knife crime had risen to the highest level in England and Wales since 2010. Of those convicted of knife crime 36% were given a prison sentence.
[3 marks — accurate point with development and exemplification]

Credit reference to aspects of the following:
- rise in violent crime
- increasing street violence
- increase in sex offences
- growth in prison population
- increase in hate crimes
- reoffending rates

13. (a) *Candidates can be credited in a number of ways **up to a maximum of 8 marks.***

Possible approaches to answering the question:

The criminal courts in Scotland are effective because they have the power to imprison people.
[1 mark — accurate but undeveloped point]

The criminal courts in Scotland are effective because they have the power to imprison people. The three different types of courts have different sentencing powers.
[2 marks — accurate point with development]

The criminal courts in Scotland are effective because they have the power to imprison people. The three different types of courts have different sentencing powers. For example, the High Court of Justiciary can impose an unlimited fine and a life sentence in comparison to the JP court which has lesser powers. This is effective as people who commit serious crimes are suitably punished.
[4 marks — accurate point with development, exemplification and analysis]

Credit reference to aspects of the following:
- deterrence
- protecting the public
- rehabilitation, for example Drug Treatment and Testing Orders
- prevention, for example Restriction of Liberty Order — tagging/curfews
- retribution, for example Community Payback Order
- compensation
- restorative justice.

(b) *Candidates can be credited in a number of ways **up to a maximum of 8 marks.***

Possible approaches to answering the question:

The Scottish Government have introduced the Caledonian System to help tackle domestic abuse and yet domestic abuse still occurs.
[1 mark — accurate but undeveloped point]

The Scottish Government have introduced the Caledonian System to help tackle domestic abuse and yet domestic abuse still occurs. The Caledonian System works with men who have been convicted of domestic abuse.

[2 marks — accurate point with development]

The Scottish Government have introduced the Caledonian System to help tackle domestic abuse and yet domestic abuse still occurs. The Caledonian System works with men who have been convicted of domestic abuse. Despite this, 51,104 domestic abuse incidents were reported to police forces across Scotland 2015–2016. The government committed £245 million to tackle domestic abuse in 2015–2016 yet between 2016–2017 domestic abuse incidents had risen to 58,810.

[4 marks — accurate point with development, exemplification and analysis]

Credit reference to aspects of the following:
- Government response of fewer short-term prison sentences
  - short-term prison sentences are still high
  - reoffending rates remain high
- mentors in violence prevention programme — violent crime has increased
- building Safer Communities Programme — not successful for all communities
- removal of Drug Courts
- alcohol related initiatives — alcohol related crime remains high
- London knife crime strategy has been unsuccessful — increase in knife crime.

14. *Candidates can be credited in a number of ways **up to a maximum of 10 marks.***

Possible approaches to answering the question:

Evidence to support Ivy Jackson's view that enough support is being provided to reduce reoffending

Source 1 highlights that 'If used, the charities which offer support for released prisoners have excellent success rates at reducing reoffending'.

[1 mark — accurate use of Source 1 but minimal development]

Source 1 highlights that 'If used, the charities which offer support for released prisoners have excellent success rates at reducing reoffending'. This is backed up in Source 2 where it states that '78% of offenders who receive this support successfully stay out of jail'.

[2 marks — accurate use of Source 1 and Source 2 linking two pieces of evidence]

Source 1 highlights that 'If used, the charities which offer support for released prisoners have excellent success rates at reducing reoffending'. This is backed up in Source 2 where it states that '78% of offenders who receive this support successfully stay out of jail'. This shows that the majority of offenders who access available support are less likely to reoffend.

[3 marks — accurate information linked from two sources with some evaluation of the information, that is 'this shows …']

Credit reference to aspects of the following:
- they can provide advice and support as to how to access state benefits and also support ex-prisoners back into education and training, giving them a better chance at staying on the straight and narrow (Source 1)

- one-to-one mentoring has been shown to turn people away from crime by helping them address practical or personal problems, such as relationship issues, accessing housing or healthcare, or finding training or work (Source 2)
- supporting people to overcome these challenges can stop them offending in the future (Source 2)
- Turn2Us is a charity which helps prisoners turn away from crime after release. They arranged a local advisor to meet with Lauren and create an action plan for her first few months after release. This ensured she knew what she was entitled to financially and supported her on her return to a local college (Source 3)

Lauren has had a successful return to society and has not reoffended in the first five years since her release. This is due to her success at accessing available support. (Source 3)

Evidence to oppose Ivy Jackson's view that enough support is being provided to reduce reoffending

Source 1 states that 'Some prisoners on release are receiving limited support and are struggling with problems, such as no accommodation and a lack of skills and resources to start again'.

[1 mark — accurate use of Source 1 but minimal development]

Source 1 states that 'Some prisoners on release are receiving limited support and are struggling with problems, such as no accommodation and a lack of skills and resources to start again'. This is backed up in Source 3 where it states 'On his release Hamish was placed in a temporary bed and breakfast for the first two weeks …'

[2 marks — accurate use of Source 1 and Source 3 linking two pieces of evidence]

Source 1 states that 'Some prisoners on release are receiving limited support and are struggling with problems, such as no accommodation and a lack of skills and resources to start again'. This is backed up in Source 3 where it states 'On his release Hamish was placed in a temporary bed and breakfast for the first two weeks …' Source 3 also highlights that 'He has since had no support for his mental health issues …'

[3 marks — well developed point — accurate use of two sources]

Credit reference to aspects of the following:
- some prisoners have even been handed tents on leaving prison to use as their accommodation. This can then lead them to reoffending in order to survive (Source 1)
- charities are available to offer support for released prisoners however they rely on the prisoners contacting them directly. This can be difficult as many prisoners do not have access to mobile phones or the internet on their release (Source 1)
- Hamish was advised to contact Step Together, however he had no access to the internet to do so (Source 3)
- an issue with these support services provided by charities and the voluntary sector is that they rely on funding from the public (Source 1)
- funding for these services has decreased from 10·7 million in 2015 to 8·4 million in 2017. (Source 2)

Part E: World powers

15. *Candidates can be credited in a number of ways **up to a maximum of 4 marks.***

Possible approaches to answering the question:

Russia

Russia has had military influence by supporting the Assad regime in the Syrian conflict.

[1 mark — accurate but undeveloped point]

Russia has had military influence by supporting the Assad regime in the Syrian conflict. Russia carried out airstrikes against militant groups opposed to the Syrian government.

[2 marks — accurate point with development]

USA

America has military bases across the world in order to support their allies against any threat.

[1 mark — accurate but undeveloped point]

America has military bases across the world in order to support their allies against any threat. These bases ensure a rapid response to any perceived threat, for example from Russia.

[2 marks — accurate point with development]

America has military bases across the world in order to support their allies against any threat. These bases ensure a rapid response to any perceived threat, for example from Russia. In 2018, the Trump Administration had plans to build up military infrastructure in Europe to deter Russian aggression.

[3 marks — accurate point with development and exemplification]

Credit reference to aspects of the following:
- size of military
- military spending
- membership of alliances
- invasions
- military exercises
- use of veto within the UN Security Council.

16. *Candidates can be credited in a number of ways **up to a maximum of 6 marks.***

Possible approaches to answering the question:

USA

One reason why some people are more likely to experience social inequalities is discrimination.

[1 mark — accurate but undeveloped point]

One reason why some people are more likely to experience social inequalities is discrimination. Blacks are often paid less than white workers even when they do the same job.

[2 marks — accurate point with development]

One reason why some people are more likely to experience social inequalities is discrimination. Blacks are often paid less than white workers even when they do the same job. For example, in the USA, the pay gap is approximately 30%.

[3 marks — accurate point with development and exemplification]

China

One reason why some people are more likely to experience social and economic inequalities is because they live in rural areas.

[1 mark — accurate but undeveloped point]

One reason why some people are more likely to experience social and economic inequalities is because they live in rural areas. Those in the countryside make very little money from farming compared to factory workers in the cities.

[2 marks — accurate point with development]

One reason why some people are more likely to experience social and economic inequalities is because they live in rural areas. Those in the countryside make very little money from farming compared to factory workers in the cities. Those in towns, especially in Special Economic Zones, earn three times more than those in the countryside.

[3 marks — accurate point with development and exemplification]

Credit reference to aspects of the following:
- other forms of discrimination, for example sexism, racism
- variations in educational attainment
- unemployment
- crime
- lone parents
- low income/poverty
- geographical location
- poverty cycle.

17. *Candidates can be credited in a number of ways **up to a maximum of 6 marks.***

Possible approaches to answering the question:

South Africa

Blacks are more likely to participate in politics to try and bring about a change.

[1 mark — accurate but undeveloped point])

Blacks are more likely to participate in politics to try and bring about a change. They could join an interest group campaigning about an issue.

[2 marks — accurate point with development]

Blacks are more likely to participate in politics to try and bring about a change. They could join an interest group campaigning about an issue. For example, Treatment Action Campaign.

[3 marks — accurate point with development and exemplification]

Blacks are more likely to participate in politics to try and bring about a change. They could join an interest group campaigning about an issue. For example, Treatment Action Campaign. This group took the government to court to make sure pregnant women got HIV drugs.

[4 marks — accurate point with development, exemplification and analysis]

Credit reference to aspects of the following:
- voting to get their party of choice elected
- more educated
- wealthier — easier to become a candidate
- politically literate
- impact of role models
- age.

Part F: World Issues

18. *Candidates can be credited in a number of ways **up to a maximum of 4 marks.***

Possible approaches to answering the question:

Conflict — Syria

Conflict can cause people to flee their homes through fear of being killed.

[1 mark — accurate but undeveloped point]

Conflict can cause people to flee their homes through fear of being killed and they may become refugees in other countries.

[2 marks — accurate point with development]

Conflict can cause people to flee their homes through fear of being killed and they may become refugees in other countries. Many people have fled Syria through fear of ISIS and have migrated to Europe, for example to Greece.

> [3 marks — accurate point with development and exemplification]

Credit reference to aspects of the following:

Terrorism
- loss of life
- financial impact due to lack of tourism
- tighter security, for example airport checks
- increase in hate crimes.

Development
- starvation
- poor education
- poor health
- poor housing
- high crime rates.

19. *Candidates can be credited in a number of ways **up to a maximum of 6 marks**.*

Possible approaches to answering the question:

Issue — Underdevelopment in Africa

The UN has been successful because it has many specialised agencies.

> [1 mark — accurate but undeveloped point]

The UN has been successful because it has many specialised agencies. These agencies can focus on individual problems and provide aid to certain countries.

> [2 marks — accurate point with development]

The UN has been successful because it has many specialised agencies. These agencies can focus on individual problems and provide aid to certain countries. For example, UNICEF has provided malaria nets to Tanzania to tackle ill health.

> [3 marks — accurate point with development and exemplification]

Credit reference to aspects of the following:

UN
- Security Council actions
- sanctions
- peacekeeping
- role of humanitarian agencies
- willingness of member states to co-operate.

NATO
- strong military power
- use of airstrikes
- co-operation of member states.

NGOs
- less bureaucratic
- specialist workers
- community knowledge
- funding.

20. *Candidates can be credited in a number of ways **up to a maximum of 6 marks**.*

Possible approaches to answering the question:

Issue — Underdevelopment in Africa

Many African countries are underdeveloped because of corrupt governments.

> [1 mark — accurate but undeveloped point]

Many African countries are underdeveloped because of corrupt governments. They spend money on weapons rather than feeding their own people.

> [2 marks — accurate point with development]

Many African countries are underdeveloped because of corrupt governments. They misspend money rather than feeding their own people. For example, the leader of Equatorial Guinea has allowed his son to spend millions of dollars of state funds on his lavish lifestyle.

> [3 marks — accurate point with development and exemplification]

Credit reference to aspects of the following:

Terrorism
- nationalism
- revenge
- religion.

Development
- debt
- civil war
- poor health — HIV
- poor education
- trade.

21. *Candidates can be credited in a number of ways **up to a maximum of 10 marks**.*

Possible approaches to answering the question:

Option 1: elect James Peddie

IER should select James Peddie as he says in Source 1 'we need to show where all funding comes from and how the money is spent'.

> [1 mark — evidence drawn from Source 1]

IER should select James Peddie as he says in Source 1 'we need to show where all funding comes from and how the money is spent'. This is backed up in Source 3 from the Daily News when it says 'A number of international NGOs have been named and shamed for not declaring how they have spent money raised and governments are calling on leaders to change practice or face penalties'.

> [2 marks — evidence linked from Source 1 and Source 3]

IER should select James Peddie as he says in Source 1 'we need to show where all funding comes from and how the money is spent'. This is backed up in Source 3 from the Daily News when it says 'A number of international NGOs have been named and shamed for not declaring how they have spent money raised and governments are calling on leaders to change practice or face penalties' and Source 2 which shows that the misuse of funds is the main concern for IER members.

> [3 marks — evidence linked from all three Sources]

Credit reference to aspects of the following:
- under-development in Africa: James Peddie says that IER have a responsibility to not just meet short-term issues within these countries but to also ensure the long-term development of these countries (Source 1) and over 50% believe that underdevelopment in Africa should be a priority for governments and NGOs (Source 3)
- specialist workers are in short supply as it is often dangerous and difficult to get time off their own work (Source 3) and there is also a huge need to modernise the organisation to use modern technology to allow specialist workers to communicate with other countries without the need to travel or take extended periods of time off (Source 1)

- the IER is a vital international organisation that is in need of an experienced and knowledgeable leader (Source 1) and James Peddie is 'Former head of Belgium's Department for Foreign Aid and Ambassador for IER in Europe'. (Source 1)

Reasons for rejecting the other option:

I rejected option 2, Elizabeth Sharp, as she said she would prioritise emergency relief in conflict zones (Source 1) but more IER members agreed that underdevelopment in Africa should be a priority. (Source 2)
  [2 marks — evidence linked from Source 1 and Source 2]

Option 2: elect Elizabeth Sharp

IER should select Elizabeth Sharp as she says 'My experience in business will help to ensure the operation of IER is efficient and effective worldwide'.
  [1 mark — evidence drawn from Source 1]

IER should select Elizabeth Sharp as she says 'My experience in business will help to ensure the operation of IER is efficient and effective worldwide'. This is supported in Source 3 when the news article says 'A US Senator criticised NGOs as being wasteful and inefficiently run, claiming that if they were run as businesses they would be more effective in delivering on their promises'.
  [2 marks — evidence linked from Source 1 and Source 3]

IER should select Elizabeth Sharp as she says 'My experience in business will help to ensure the operation of IER is efficient and effective worldwide'. This is supported in Source 3 when the news article says 'A

US Senator has criticised NGOs as being wasteful and inefficiently run, claiming that if they were run as businesses they would be more effective in delivering on their promises'. This is further shown in the pie chart in Source 2 as 35% of members are concerned about efficiency/effectiveness.
  [3 marks — evidence linked from all three Sources]

Credit reference to aspects of the following:
- many areas across the globe need access to specialist workers who have the expertise to give advice on how best to take actions to reduce the impact of man-made or natural events and to help areas devastated recover (Source 3) and we need to ensure that more workers are sent to crisis areas and use their expertise to improve the situation immediately. IER would employ these specialist workers full-time to avoid clashes with other jobs (Source 1)
- emergency relief in conflict zones: with increasing need for emergency relief in areas where conflict has had a huge impact on the local population, this should be a priority for IER (Source 1) and a majority of people said they agreed or strongly agreed that emergency relief in conflict zones should be a priority. (Source 2)

Reasons for rejecting the other option:

I rejected option 1 because James Peddie says 'Women's Rights: Ensuring women have equal access to all areas of life and work across the globe' should be a priority but Source 2 shows that this has the highest number of people disagreeing in comparison to the other priorities.
  [2 marks — evidence linked from Source 1 and Source 2]